SIGNPOSTS FOR CIVVY STREET

SIGNPOSTS
FOR CIVVY STREET

A comprehensive and detailed
guide for all Service Leavers
and veterans

DR KAREN CASTLE AND RICHY KELLY

Editing, Design, typesetting and publishing by UK Book Publishing
www.ukbookpublishing.com

ISBN: 978-1-914195-51-8

CONTENTS

ACKNOWLEDGEMENTS

We owe several people a debt of gratitude for their support and contributions to this book. Each of the veterans who provided frank and honest case studies that enabled us to develop discussions and narrative around some important issues of resettlement deserve our sincere thanks.

Dan Jarvis MBE MP offered detailed support and advice specifically on matters concerning finance, health and well-being and immigration. We are incredibly thankful.

Authors: Dr Karen Castle and Richy Kelly

DEDICATION

This book is dedicated to Jocky, a humble and modest Airborne Soldier who fought at Arnhem in 1944. He made the transition from soldier to civilian and back again. He was forever proud of his life in the Parachute Regiment and of all his military experiences. Jocky was just 21 years of age when he fought, putting his life on the line for our freedom, many miles from his home. On his return, he met and accomplished another challenge – adapting to life on Civvy Street. Jocky – Never Forgotten.

AUTHORS' BIOGRAPHY

Karen trained as a nurse and after qualifying and working in the NHS for several years she joined Her Majesty's Prison Service. She completed her prison officer training and served in several prisons across the UK as a prison hospital officer. As one of the first ever female officers to work in male prison establishments, she spent several years on detachments to prisons in London and other areas of the UK. Whilst in the Prison service she studied and researched mental and emotional health issues in prisoners and became interested in the plight of military veterans who were serving time in prison. On leaving the prison service, she found resettlement on Civvy Street challenging as health employers were reluctant to employ her after her extended period out of the civilian workplace. She took a college certificate in education, followed by undergraduate and post graduate degrees, and has never looked back. She has worked as a staff nurse, nursing sister and matron before swapping the hospital wards for a classroom and has spent the last 15 years as a university tutor after having successfully obtained her Doctorate in Education. Karen is currently a senior lecturer at Staffordshire University in the Staffordshire Business School. She has significant experience and understanding of supporting military veterans and civilian adult learners who are returning to learning and who are seeking career changes. She has also been responsible for recruiting and appointing staff to various positions both in the private and public sector.

Richy served for 22 years in the Parachute Regiment of the British Army. During this time, he served on operational tours in Northern Ireland, Kosovo and Iraq, and on numerous exercises across Europe, USA, Belize and Kenya. Prior to him completing his army service, he was the recruiting sergeant at an Army careers office. He found this role most rewarding as it offered him the valuable opportunity of learning what was happening on Civvy Street. He credits this job with enabling him to come to terms with managing the various and significant challenges to adapting to civilian life. Since leaving the army, Richy has worked in corporate recruitment, and more recently with the Army Reserves, two roles that have provided him with invaluable insight into the complex situation of where the military and civilian workforce meet. Richy has various recruitment and welfare qualifications, as well as several military medals; he also has a Diploma in personal training and nutrition. Richy has more recently been able to draw on these military experiences and qualifications to offer practical expertise to inform his work with the army reserves. Richy's military experience and his current involvement in several military networks has been invaluable in the critical development of this book. He is currently a recruitment co-ordinator with the British Army.

CHAPTER 1

INTRODUCTION

There are over 145 thousand personnel serving in the British armed forces, over half of which are in the British Army (Clark 2020) and around 15,000 – 20,000 people leave the armed forces each year (Buswell 2020). Some of these military veterans have a future life and career planned and organised, but many do not. There are also an estimated 2.4 million UK Armed forces veterans in Great Britain (Office for Veterans Affairs 2020), several of whom apparently still struggle with life on Civvy Street. This handbook has been developed both for military personnel going through the resettlement phase of their service or who have recently left the armed forces, and for veterans who have left the military some time previously. It is intended to be a practical handbook that offers information and guidance in a pragmatic and straightforward manner to support you in helping to build your confidence in exploring options when resettling or living on Civvy Street.

"For ex service personnel and their families looking to transition into civilian life, there are 3 important aspects: Health, housing and hard work. All sides must be in balance, a virtual and virtuous equilateral triangle. Get them right and you maximise the chances of a successful and sustainable transition."

Air Vice-Marshall Ray Lock CBE. In veterans Work (2018) moving on. Downloaded from veteranswork.org.uk

In this introduction we offer a rationale for the book and give some suggestions of how you might find it beneficial to use the book. The objectives are outlined, and each chapter is explored to offer a brief overview of the theme of the chapter. You are encouraged to consider your military experience and skills, reflecting critically on these whilst reading the book, particularly when considering any plans for civilian training and further education or a new career. You only leave the forces once; this handbook offers some signposts and suggestions to make this *once in a lifetime* event a little easier.

We use a practical approach throughout the book and particularly in terms of providing references and signposts to other reading material or services. There is a reference section at the end of each chapter, which contains the details of the resources that we have used to support our discussions within that chapter but will also be useful to you in following up anything that is of particular interest to you. These are by no means the only sources of information on any of the subjects – we don't claim to be providing the names of all the charities and organisations that are available. But we do offer a sample of the sorts of information and advice that is out there.

In 2014 a major review on armed forces transition and resettlement was reported. The Veterans' Transition Review by Lord Ashcroft (2014) argues that on joining the service, young service personnel are ready to be deployed anywhere they are ordered, totally committed to tasks, and prepared to give their lives for the mission. The Ashcroft review goes on to point out that many of those responsible in the services do not place transition or resettlement high enough on the agenda, preferring to consider that it is the armed forces' duty to fight rather than prepare for civilian life. This is backed up by the discussions we had with veterans during the development of the book, many of whom felt they had not had appropriate or sufficient support to prepare them for life on Civvy Street. During the development of this book, we spoke to several veterans and people who have recently been through resettlement or are currently going through resettlement in each of the armed forces. This was to enable the information to be authentic and based on real-life stories. Some of these conversations are presented as vignette case studies and have both informed the content of the book and enabled us to focus on certain key areas that we felt it necessary to explore in more depth.

RATIONALE

The research we carried out prior to compiling this book led us to believe that significant numbers of people leaving the armed forces struggle with the transition to civilian life. Similarly, some military veterans who have been out of the forces for several years, still seem to be experiencing challenges in terms of living and working in Civvy Street. The struggles they encounter range from housing and finance challenges to finding suitable employment. Some service leavers suffer from significant emotional and mental health problems, and these sometimes create barriers to them resettling into Civvy Street. After serving in the military, working age veterans are nearly twice as likely as civilians to be unemployed (Royal British Legion 2019). The reasons for these are of course complex and vary between each veteran. However, we found that there are some general barriers that seem to be creating challenges for many service leavers. These barriers seem to be particularly visible in circumstances when service leavers have attempted to gain access to advice and guidance on what services are available for veterans. There also seems to be some misunderstanding and ambiguity in terms of access to further and higher education and particularly when service personnel have sought civilian employment. There are several areas of resettlement where we feel service leavers may benefit from support; we argue that having time to reflect on your own personal experiences and situation and, most importantly in seeking specialised help and guidance when and as necessary, is paramount to your successful transfer to civilian life.

OBJECTIVES

Therefore, this book will look at different aspects of resettlement and offer some suggestions on how you may address any areas that provide barriers to a successful transition. We felt compelled to put together this resource to support you in your quest to re-establish yourself in the various aspects of life on Civvy Street. We also wanted to provide a resource for veterans who are relatively established on Civvy Street, albeit still finding difficulties with some aspects of life out of the military. You are each highly skilled and talented individuals whose military experiences will be invaluable to some civilian employers. Similarly, you may wish to utilise your military learning credits to access academic or training courses. We pick up on these areas and explore some of the options and signpost you to advice services that are available. As the "only mandatory element of resettlement for a service leaver is the resettlement advisory brief (RAB) usually delivered by a resettlement officer" (Veterans Gateway 2020), we believe this book will be invaluable to all service leavers and veterans as a portal for information and as a handbook to support and inform decisions regarding your future in Civvy Street. We are aware that there is a significant amount of resettlement information in circulation, but we understand from conversations we have had with service leavers and veterans, that this is sometimes difficult to understand and is, in some cases, challenging to access.

The main objective of this handbook is to complement any military resettlement and transition programmes and courses. It is not our intention to compete with these or any distinct programmes developed by specialist charities and organisations to support service leavers and veterans. We want to provide you with a source of information that will enable you to embrace these programmes and to discover, for yourself, the information and services that you are entitled to. From our research and from the literature review we carried out prior to planning this book, we identified some key areas of concerns from service leavers, veterans and from other researchers in the field. This handbook will address some of these and provide some suggestions and practical guidance on how to use the vast diverse experience and skills you have built up whilst in the military.

Some of the veterans and service leavers we spoke to felt that their voice wasn't being heard on Civvy Street. They spoke of being "fobbed off" by some of the charities that they thought were supposed to help them. Some spoke of feeling "let down" and "passed from pillar to post". We understand that resettlement is challenging and that, having not been working in Civvy Street, you may find some events and situations difficult. Many of the civilians you interact with, some in management or senior positions, may not realise your struggles or challenges, so may come across as not really understanding you or having any consideration for your plight. In this book, we have attempted to offer you some information and guidance that is relevant and useful to you. But you may need to be assertive and persistent in your communication and in chasing up and asking for information and advice. There are some areas of society that will absolutely get your case and will go out of their way to support and help, but there are others that won't and it's in these areas that you'll need to draw on your previous (military) skills of resilience, assertiveness, and effective communication to put across your case.

Being in the forces is often felt like being part of an exceptionally large family with a shared sense of discipline, comradeship, team spirit and purpose. In civilian occupations there is most likely, not the same sense of togetherness or team spirit. For some this is the biggest hurdle to try to overcome, and for others, it could feature as a significant barrier to further training or employment. We have acknowledged this throughout the book. We understand that the Ministry of Defence's Career Transition Partnership (CTP) programme provides resettlement support to eligible service leavers and we hope this book goes some way to supporting the journey through any CTP programmes that you access. But we also feel that it is a useful handbook to support you through the early stages of any training and development and employment, either military or civilian.

There is a plethora of information on resettlement available, but it seems this is quite dispersed and not always readily accessible. We hope this handbook goes some way to address this, in bringing together some key contacts and services in one place. Make the most and the best of your resettlement and find out what you are entitled to. We discuss some of the benefits that you may be able to access in the book, but you should also research your own individual entitlements. Some of the main organisations, charities and advice services that help you are included in the book, but we urge you to seek out all the guidance and information you can in order that you give yourself the best possible chance of a successful resettlement.

It has been argued that a research gap is evident in terms of under-standing UK Service leaver resilience and resettlement, for example, the Forces in Mind trust commissioned RAND Europe to carry out a literature review of service leaver resilience through transition as it was believed if service leavers demonstrated a strong "resilience" they would transition out of the forces more effectively that those who did not. Resilience in this context referring to: positively handing change, coping with uncertainty, and managing issues associated with transition. However, the RAND research discovered a more negative aspect, as the "can do" attitude and self-belief embedded in the minds and lives of military personnel whilst serving acts as a barrier to seeking support once they leave the service. Many veterans feel too proud to seek support and help, and this has prevented them from approaching or self-referring to any of the charities. There also seems to be a feeling amongst some service leavers that they somehow don't fit into civilian life, that civilian colleagues and managers won't understand them. This is something that can create a feeling of "us and them" which won't help anyone in the resettlement process. We pick up on the civilian employers' responsibilities to military veterans in one of our other books, but we'll begin some discussion around this later in this handbook when we analyse these feelings and provide some discussion that comes out of the case studies.

New organisations supporting veterans and service leavers are being established all the time and the best advice we can give is to carry out your own searches and research to determine the best source of help for yourself. We hope to provide here, in this book, some signposts to some of the key organisations and charities. But a good place to start would be to explore which organisations and businesses have signed the Armed Forces Covenant, a promise by some organisations across the nation to ensure those who have served the Country and their families are treated fairly. The covenant supports serving personnel, service leavers, veterans and their families and is a pledge that thousands of businesses and organisation have committed to. Organisations that have signed the Armed Forces Covenant have done so because they want to support the military and veterans; these organisations are therefore likely to understand some of the complexities and challenges that service leavers and veterans face when resettling and when seeking employment. So, in understanding which organisations have signed up to the covenant, gives you a good start in knowing where you may get appropriate and relevant support and advice.

This handbook is divided into chapters with a focus on a particular area of resettlement. The discussions and suggestions we put forward are not meant to be the complete list of topics on a particular area, as these change daily, but we have set out some priority areas for you to explore further. We hope you will find the book easy to follow and useful. The chapters can be read independently as stand- alone sections, but you might benefit from reading the book in its entirety.

Chapter 2 offers some real-life stories from service leavers and veterans from each of the armed forces. We carried out discussions whilst researching this handbook, both from people who had secured civilian employment and training places, and from those who were self-employed. We also spoke to people who had not sought employment, for one reason or another. We had conversations with service leavers and veterans who have been diagnosed with Post Traumatic Stress Disorder and other emotional conditions, and those with physical injuries sustained because of their service. We hope that by us sharing some poignant stories and experiences from ex-military personnel, you will be able to relate to the issues, situations and events that are expressed, and reflect on how you could benefit from learning from these vignettes. In this chapter the stories are set out as separate case studies, but we draw on the conversations throughout the book.

Chapter 3 looks at some of the issues with respect to housing that some people leaving the forces are faced with. We discuss some of the considerations around renting and buying properties. There is information and guidance available from charities and local authorities, and we mention these whilst discussing the issues in more depth. We explore the practice of engaging with estate agents, letting agents and solicitors, and offer some practical suggestions for you to consider when making decisions regarding finding a home. We have drawn on information from civilian estate and rental agents in the completion of this chapter.

Chapter 4. Some service leavers experience significant financial difficulties and challenges when they leave the military. In this chapter, we discuss pensions and how your military pension may be affected if you engage in further work. We also look at welfare and benefits, and we list some of the benefits you may be entitled to claim. We discuss the issue of debt and offer signposts to some of the organisations and support networks that offer guidance on debt. Loans and financial support are also analysed, and we discuss the limitations of pay day loans. We have drawn on information from legal and financial experts, and from information from the Forces Pension Society columns printed in several *The Pathfinder* magazines.

Chapter 5: In this chapter we address some of the sensitivities around health and wellbeing. It is reasonably well documented that some service leavers experience emotional and mental health problems when they leave the military. In this chapter we acknowledge this as we discuss various charities and organisations that exist to support with mental health issues. Once you leave the military, your health needs are catered for by the NHS. There are an increasing number of GPs and medical centres that are becoming "Veteran friendly". This means that staff from these centres have attended training informing them of the needs of military veterans. This chapter offers some suggestions of how you might find an NHS medical practitioner. We have drawn on information contained on the NHS website and from specialist charities to inform our discussions in this chapter.

Chapter 6. This chapter gives you the opportunity to identify your own Learning Style according to the Honey and Mumford learning styles questionnaire. Once you have established this, you will be able to understand which courses and which methods of learning may suit you best. The chapter examines what critical and reflective learning is and how critical analysis can be used to support your learning. You will have done this many times during your service, you may just not have realised it, but most college and all university courses require you to develop as a critical learner to some extent. You will be encouraged to critically explore your own learning opportunities. We look at what skills are required for you to be a critical learner. "Critical" in this sense is not a negative term, but rather is the concept of consideration and balance, and not taking anything at face value but instead, asking questions and thinking around the subject. This may be something new to you, as in the military, you may have been discouraged from asking too many questions, or challenging decisions and views. Critical learning requires you to do just that, ask questions, consider the options, and think about alternatives. This chapter also grapples with the notion of reflection and reflecting in and on action. It offers the opportunity for you to explore the concept of reflection and how this can inform learning and knowledge development. This chapter explores the notion of prior experiential and certificated learning. Prior experiential learning is essentially drawn from those experiences you had whilst serving that led you to understanding something more, or the mistakes you made or witnessed that enabled you to understand something more fully or in more detail. You may have learnt something about yourself through some adversity that you'd put to the back of your mind, or that you'd not thought was worth remembering. We encourage you to reflect on these experiences to draw out some skills you may have hidden until now. Most colleges and universities offer a *recognition of prior learning* access route to courses, so it might be useful to understand how the practical learning and experience you had whilst working in military service can be used to support your application to college or university courses. Some of these courses may have certificates awarded for assessment, but others may not. Chapter 6 offers some ideas for you to consider how you might use your prior experience or certificated learning to access civilian training. It also encourages you to reflect on your work experiences in terms of how you worked as part of a team and how you worked alone, and how these methods of working can inform your learning and development. The chapter will also discuss how prior learning can be recognised by higher education establishments as access to degree programmes.

Chapter 7. This chapter follows on closely from the previous one and is about preparing for Further and Higher Education. Here the focus is on the skills and techniques needed to apply for and begin a college or university course. This could be undergraduate or postgraduate, or a vocational programme such as an apprenticeship. The chapter will address the study skills necessary for further and higher education and will equip you with the tools needed to embark on further training. A lot of what we are trying to do in this chapter is to provide you with information and suggestion to enable you to be confident in learning in a different way to that which you have done before. Your skill set will probably be there already, it merely needs tweaking.

Chapter 8. This chapter looks at the civilian workplace and provides a discussion around the civilian workplace culture. It offers the opportunity to reflect on different occupational areas and compare how the culture differs to that in the military. It is a useful chapter in offering you a context for transition into a civilian role. We have learned from talking to several veterans who are now in civilian employment that employers differ greatly in how they seem to consider ex-military personnel. We have also spoken to employers and asked their opinion of employing veterans. These opinions have underpinned our discussions in this chapter.

Chapter 9. In this chapter we provide the opportunity to consider how to prepare for a different career. Embarking on a new career can be daunting for many people, but for people who have spent many years in the military it can feel particularly challenging. We will discuss some of the challenges but also some of the many opportunities that are well suited to ex-forces personnel. This chapter will suggest how a good curriculum vitae might look. It will explore what employers want when they ask for a covering letter for a vacant post, and then it will suggest important considerations of the job interview. Employment skills will, of course, vary according to the specific type of occupation, but we argue that there are certain skills required in most organisations, for example, communication and collaboration, recognition of equality and diversity, awareness of professional and statutory bodies. We mentioned earlier that whilst serving you were trained to be ready and willing to fight. You were, and still are, disciplined to certain regimes and routines. Civvy Street is quite different.

Civilian occupational areas and businesses have different cultures, you are likely to be more comfortable in some rather than others, so knowing and understanding something of the culture of your potential new employment could be useful. For example, state schools generally have quite a liberal culture, embracing difference and diversity, promoting open speech and are nurturing environments, whereas a blue-chip business organisation is likely to be more progressive with targets and deadlines that, it is argued, require a more structured and directive approach. This chapter will also explore how ex-forces personnel are sometimes perceived by civilian employers and will offer suggestions and methods for any stereotypes to be challenged. Case studies will be used from ex-military personnel who have been employed by civilian employers and their views will be critically examined. Case study evidence is also used to demonstrate how some service leavers have felt when embarking on new careers. This chapter will discuss these skills and others in the context of career development.

Chapter 10. This is a summary of the key resettlement elements that have been discussed within the book. We bring together some of the significant considerations that we were informed were creating the challenges to service leavers. The book ends with an epilogue dedicated to Chris, one of the veterans who supported the development of the book and whose story of resettlement informed the book greatly. Chris sadly died before the book was published.

SOME INITIAL SIGNPOSTS

Throughout this book we offer signposts to some of the organisations and charities that support and help military veterans and service leavers with information and guidance; to the best of our knowledge, the contact details of these are correct at the time this book was published. These are by no means the only organisations; there are new businesses and services being created all the time that focus on supporting veterans. We therefore suggest that you consider joining associations or networks with likeminded people (not necessarily all ex-military as you're attempting to resettle into civilian life). There are several ex-military organisations that you will probably benefit from joining and will enjoy sharing past experiences and reminiscing. However, there may also be several non-military organisations that may be of benefit to you. Don't dismiss these just because they are not military-focused. There are hundreds of organisations and groups, some that focus on specific interests and some that are more general, others are local to a specific area, but some are national organisations, for example: *The Round Table* club – a non-political association open to men between the ages of 18 – 45 from any profession or trade – to encourage high ethical standards in commercial life, promote fellowship amongst young professional and businessmen and to empower individuals to make a positive impact at work, at home and in the community (**www.roundtable.co.uk**). *The Rotary Club* – Provides services to others, supporting those who need it most and transforming lives. The Rotary club "sees solutions, tapping into the professional skills, expertise and knowledge of the members to make a difference". There are numerous Rotary projects and activities that you can get involved in (www.rotarygbi.org). *The Inner Wheel* is an all-female organisation that promotes friendship, encourages personal service, and fosters international understanding (**www.innerwheel.co.uk**). Joining a group such as one of these may help you in your transition to civilian life.

The following are examples of military organisations and information sources that you might find useful and from which some of the information is detailed throughout this book:

Army Families Federations – **www.aff.org.uk** The independent voice of Army families working to improve the quality of life for Army families around the world, on any aspect of life that is affected by the Army lifestyle.

Army Benevolent Fund – **www.soldierscharity.org** The national charity of the British Army providing support to soldiers, veterans, and their immediate family.

Royal Air Force Benevolent Fund – **www.rafbf.org** The RAF leading welfare charity supporting all serving and former members of the RAF as well as partners and dependent children.

Royal Naval Benevolent Trust – **www.rnbt.org.uk** Providing financial support to Royal Navy and Royal Marines personnel and their families in challenging times.

Royal Navy Association – **www.royal-naval-association.co.uk** A family of current and former Royal Naval personnel offering advice on welfare and employment matters as well as providing a support network and social events.

The Kings Centre for Military Health Research is based at King's College London and specialises in Military research. There are some interesting research reports on the website: **www.kcl.ac.uk/kcmhr**

The Veterans' transition review (2014) – Lord Ashcroft on: **www. veteranstransition.co.uk** An independent review carried out by Lord Ashcroft focusing on the process of leaving the Armed Forces and resettling to civilian life.

Service Leavers' Guide October 2020 (published by the MOD in 2012 and updated in 2020) Offering information and advice prior to and after leaving regular Military Service.

REFERENCES

Buswell, G. (2020) Can service leavers resuscitate the NHS? *Civvy Street*. Impact publishing ltd. Glasgow. ISSN 1746-8426

Clark, D. (2020) Number of Personnel in the armed forces. Statista. www.statista.com

Office for Veterans' Affairs (2020) Veterans Factsheet. www.Assets.publishing.service.gov.uk

RAND Europe (2019) *Pathfinder* magazine December 2019.

The Royal British Legion (2019) *The strategy for our Veterans*. Consultation response. Storage.rblcdn.co.uk

Trowler, P. (1996) Angels in marble? Accrediting prior experiential learning in higher education. *Studies in Higher education*. 21.1. 17–30.

Veterans Gateway. (2020) *Transitioning out of the Armed forces*. Support. veteransgateway.org.uk

CHAPTER 2

REAL LIFE STORIES

INTRODUCTION

Prior to writing this book, we interviewed several people who had served in the military and who had experienced resettlement on Civvy Street. We talked to people who had served in the British Army, the Royal Navy and the Royal Airforce. The identity of the veterans responding to this research is protected at their request, so we use just their first name or their initials. We initially wanted to learn how they experienced resettlement, what their challenges were and how they overcame these. However, some of these conversations led to other topics that we thought may be relevant to you and where this is the case, we have included them both here in this chapter and throughout the book. We have reported each of the stories as they have been told to us so that we can offer a true account of these real-life interpretations of resettlement. It is intended that these reflections and anecdotes on the resettlement stories will support your own resettlement journey and transition to Civvy Street.

RESETTLEMENT VIGNETTES

Chris – Army

Chris served in the Parachute Regiment of the British Army for 7 years. During our discussion he spoke of the camaraderie and team spirit within the Regiment and how this was very different to the team spirit he experiences in Civvy Street. During the last few months of his resettlement period, whilst still in the Army, he attended a Police Force career conference as he was always interested in becoming a civilian police officer. The police force that he applied to, had a "ban on ex-Military personnel applying to the police, but that ban had been lifted" prior to him applying. He went through the application process, thinking he needed more qualifications than he had so was surprised when he was informed that he'd been selected for Police officer training. He successfully completed his training, adapting, he felt, very well to the different language and humour within the Police Force. He subsequently served in the police force in the UK from 1997, so amassing a service of 24 years. Chris wasn't aware of his entitlement to any learning credits that were available to him during and post resettlement – had he have been aware of these at the time, he thought he may well have used them to complete a degree that would support his police career. He felt overall that his resettlement was very straightforward. He said that the fact he'd been in the Army had helped him to get into the police force. The tragedy for us is that Chris sadly passed away during the completion of this book. The Epilogue is dedicated to him – Chris – RIP.

Matt – Army

Matt told us that his resettlement was very straightforward and he didn't feel that it was problematic. He attended a 2-week resettlement course that was run by civilians at an Army Education Centre. He thought, at the time, that the course was particularly good and had started to prepare him for some of the things he would encounter on Civvy Street. However, he wasn't aware of the learning credits that he could have had access to had he wanted to obtain any civilian qualifications that would have helped him in Civvy Street. He initially worked in a security job for a major retail company before applying for and being accepted into the Fire Service. He said that at first, the fire service did not encourage ex-forces personnel into the service as many didn't have a degree, but that this practice has changed and now the brigade accepts military veterans. He is still a fire fighter today and believes that his military training and experience has been invaluable to him in Civvy Street.

Paul – RAF

During Paul's last 12 months in the RAF he was told of several "job fairs" for people going through resettlement in various locations up and down the country, but due to his work commitments (which the RAF had directed him to complete), he was not able to get to any of these. He was aware of the learning credits but said that they had to be used on "trade related" training programmes, none of which were applicable to him, so he didn't use any of his credits. He attended a "housing brief" during his final 12 months and was informed that unless he moved to the north of the UK, there was very little help. It was suggested to him that he "went down the Local Authority route". Paul felt many RAF service personnel go into private rental properties as he had done himself. He was aware of the tax-free loan that was available to help to buy a house. His view was that the RAF offered the opportunities but "you had to work them out yourself and had to do it all yourself". Paul did get a civilian job via the job search site indeed **www.indeed.co.uk**. This job, that he still has today, is a similar driving and transport job that he had whilst in the military and he is based at the same military station that he worked at previously. Paul said on several occasions throughout the conversation that the services are reactive instead of being proactive when it comes to resettlement. His view was that "once you are out there on Civvy Street, there is no safety net". He was aware of SSAFA, the RAFBF, but said that he was "largely on my own in the end" doing everything for himself and getting information from different sources. He said, "you have to be very strong".

Al – Army

Al joined the Royal Corps of Transport (later to become the Royal Logistic corps) in 1986. After spending 18 years in the British Army, he went through resettlement in 2004. Al felt that he had been lucky as he had several friends already in Civvy Street and who were able to help him. But he said there are many pitfalls for people going through resettlement who don't have Civvy Street contacts, those who went into the military at 17 or 18 years of age and for whom the military is all that they have known. He said that some of the squaddies think Civvy Street is remarkably like the Army – "they don't realise that if you want anything doing, you have to do it yourself."

Al said that he thought there was an "overkill of staff" in the Army compared to Civvy Street, where "you have to do several jobs at the same time and there's only you to do it". In the Army, there's a sense that you only have one job to do, and this is different in civilian employment, where you are likely to have several responsibilities assigned to your role. But for Al, the biggest problem is that there is nowhere to get the practical help you need before you are discharged. He used several examples of where people have just needed someone to talk to in terms of what they need to do to find somewhere to live, or how to get employment, but he stressed that there is no structured process for supporting people when leaving. This results in confusion and frustration when military leavers find themselves on Civvy Street, thinking they'll get help to do things and find things out but, they have to do it themselves. He also sounded a warning in terms of the use of social media and thought that much of social media is not helpful to ex-military personnel as there is a lot of negativity towards people who have served in the armed forces. He said that this, as well as other issues, for example, applying for jobs and understanding the civilian workplace "hits you in the face" when you first come out of the services as it's the "biggest culture shock" anyone could experience.

Jane – QA. Army

Jane said that her resettlement was very straightforward, she was a qualified nurse when she went into the army, so it was "relatively easy" to get a job when she came out. Jane is a qualified mental health nurse, so her qualifications were sought after on Civvy Street. She was only aware of the training credits as her husband was in the RAF and going through resettlement at the same time and he knew about them so was able to tell her. Jane spoke of feeling a bit like a "duck out of water" when she first started working in an NHS hospital. She said that although the "nursing language" was similar, she missed the "military banter and humour". Jane spoke of a lack of discipline amongst some of her civilian colleagues. However, she spoke of a culture in the military of managers being able to "talk to you however they liked, shouting and being aggressive". She said that "my managers in the Civvy hospital just wouldn't get away with it". Jane was living in a private rental property with her husband, and they were incredibly happy. However, she did "regret not getting on the housing ladder" when she had the opportunity several years ago. Jane had cause to contact one of the armed forces charities during her resettlement but felt that the charity was not as helpful as she had hoped and "ended up doing most of the finding out" herself.

Phil – Navy

Phil had been a Petty Officer in the Royal Navy for 25 years. He left the navy in 2010. Phil had four children, so to support them financially, he wanted to get a civilian job as soon as possible after leaving the Navy. He already had a house, and his family were settled into schools in Hampshire so he didn't want to uproot them to move to accommodate his work. He felt, therefore, that his choices were either to take a job out of the area and for him to live away from the family, or to settle for a local job that would mean he could spend more time with his children. Phil had been an electronics specialist whilst in the Navy so thought he'd have a better chance of a job on Civvy Street if he "stuck to what" he knew. However, he soon realised that civilian jobs of a similar nature to those within the Navy were hard to come by and the more he looked for a job that echoed that of his Naval role, the more he became frustrated when he couldn't find one. He talked of becoming quite difficult to live with as he felt that he's lost "all status and identity" that he had in his PO post in the Navy. There were tensions in his marriage that led to his divorce. Phil said that with the hindsight he now has, he should have sought specialist career advice from a civilian organisation rather than a Naval perspective, as he thought this would have given him a better indication of what civilian employers wanted and also would have informed him of how he could make best use of his electronics qualifications.

Phil had several local jobs following his resettlement, which included: working for a security alarm company, working for the local authority and as a researcher for a communications company. He then took out a franchise which he said he was ill prepared for in terms of what to expect from that type of employment. He claims to have "lost too much money" on the franchise, so in the end he decided to "just get an ordinary job that paid enough to cover my rent and to take the kids out" when he saw them. He is now working for a shop fitting company as an electrical specialist and says it's the "best thing he has ever done". He talks of feeling a freedom that he has not experienced for a long time and he enjoys "the banter" with the other workers within the company. He wanted to offer some advice to anyone thinking of taking out a franchise. The advice is: "do your homework on the franchise company; make absolutely sure you know what costs you will incur and if there are any hidden costs – including the franchise company's cut of your profits – make sure you understand any penalties you need to pay if you end the franchise agreement and get everything signed under a legal contract.

Lawrie – Army

Lawrie served 10 years in the Army before being medically discharged. He has PTSD, anxiety and depression and admits to not really wanting to talk to me (Karen) at first as I wasn't a military veteran. When I asked him to explain why he felt it inappropriate to talk to a civilian, he thought for a while before saying that he preferred to "stick to conversations with people who would know what he was going through". He did say that he thought I was very brave, trying to get military veterans to speak to me as he thought most ex-forces personnel are "much happier" talking to other military veterans rather than civilians. He didn't think many civilians were "sympathetic" to military or ex-military Veterans. He was in regular touch with one of the military charities that help service leavers, and he has regular meetings with representatives from the charity that he says "helps a bit –sometimes". He is getting counselling for his mental health problems and has recently registered for an NHS practitioner. Lawrie said he hadn't had any "useful" help whilst going through resettlement and this led to him having to find his own way. He struggled to make any civilian friends as "they" didn't understand him and "didn't seem to want to get to know him". I asked him what he thought the military should do to make the resettlement transition more effective; he thought for a while before saying "anything would be better than what they do now".

RM – Army

Most people in the forces become accustomed through training and conditioning to accept and 'deal' with a dark and blunt type of humour or comments etc. known as 'Banter' and it serves the purpose to help deal with incredibly stressful and demanding times, dealing with adversity, and laughing in the face of danger etc. Also, most forces personnel know each other intimately as they spend far more time, working, living, and sharing accommodation with each other, so know the limits and what a person will react to and what is a touchy subject. But displaying this type of humour with their civvy work-colleagues, whom they don't have this type of relationship with, is very much different.

"I was running Personal Training and Fitness sessions in a local Army Reserve Centre; all of the class were civilians who wanted to experience a workout in a military style method and environment etc. The Reserve Centre was manned by Regular Army Permanent Staff and one of them, a Warrant Officer, decided to look at who was coming into the session even though it was nothing to do with him. I can only imagine why he might have wanted to look at who was attending the session. As two young ladies were entering the class he commented: 'here's the Ugly Sisters!' Why he made this comment was beyond anyone and fortunately I knew the two ladies and managed to defuse the situation by talking to them, informing them that this was inappropriate behaviour etc. etc. This sort of comment may well be accepted in the Military with people you know well, but it is absolutely not acceptable in this context (or any other, for that matter) on Civvy Street."

Karl – Army

Karl spent 10 years in the Parachute regiment. He said initially that his resettlement was "relaxed" largely since he was UK-based. He said that he had to "do all the paperwork" himself and had to "fit any resettlement activities and events around the army schedule"; this led to him missing several events that he felt would have been beneficial. He felt that because he "had a good boss who allowed him to sort things" for his resettlement, it "wasn't too bad" for him. He said he thought it "all comes down to the type of boss you have". However, he didn't have a particularly effective education officer: whenever Karl wanted to see him or speak with him about resettlement issues, he was "never in or never available". Karl used his learning credits to do a close protection course and a maritime course/water security and said that he "had to sort everything out, the paperwork and admin for these courses" himself. Karl said that once he had left and the first steps he took on Civvy Street were "really scary and when the penny dropped that I was not in the army anymore thought what have I done? Can I get back in [the Army]?", he was offered a job with a security firm that would mean he would be oversees and so he started to feel that he was "getting somewhere". However, there were problems within the company and the job fell through, which left Karl out of work. He was unemployed for three months, which led to him feeling even more vulnerable and scared. These feelings were emphasised greatly when he realised that advice he took (from a fellow colleague) regarding investing his pension was incorrect and, as it turns out, seemingly "very dodgy". Karl appealed to us to stress to you to think very carefully before transferring your pension. He said to make sure you only deal with accredited and credible financial companies that are transparent in terms of what they are doing with your pension. He is still fighting to get his pension sorted, but now has some support from a credible source in doing this. Karl said that he is aware that his story is not unique, both in terms of resettlement issues and in terms of the pension issues. He said that "when you're in the Army, aggression is rewarded, that's one of the reasons so many people coming out struggle on Civvy Street", as the Army "don't teach you how to manage this aggression that they have built up in you so that you can cope with situations appropriately on Civvy Street". Karl is settled for now in a job that enables him to provide for his family, but he is keen to use his remaining learning credits on a degree course that will enable him to get a better job in the future.

SUMMARY

There are some themes that have occurred after discussing resettlement with these military veterans. For example, the notion that during resettlement and once you've left the forces, you need to chase things up yourself and complete documentation and administrative tasks yourself, that there is no one in Civvy Street to do this for you. This is probably true; Civvy Street doesn't have an "admin section" or something like that which you can go to for help, so it's largely down to you to manage your own affairs. Getting help from experienced and qualified people will help massively, and we hope that this book will go some way to signposting you to some of these people and agencies. Another theme is the notion of feeling vulnerable once you've left the service. It's hardly surprising really, given the job you've had and the structure of the military; Civvy Street doesn't have that sort of structure and so it's easy to feel exposed and scared. Joining an association or organisation (not necessarily as an employee) might help you to feel part of something, though it would be difficult to replicate the feeling of togetherness that the military fosters. The rest of the book is divided into sections that are largely based on the main issues that veterans have told us are the key issues when resettling. There was also a sense that the sooner you start planning your resettlement, ideally before your discharge, the better. The veterans we spoke to alluded to resettlement being a culture shock; again, this is no surprise really, given the life you've been leading previously in the military, but that's just it, isn't it? *Previously* - now your life is in a different context, a civilian context, and you can draw on these discussions here and your own experiences in making your future life successful and enjoyable.

CHAPTER 3

HOUSING

INTRODUCTION

One of the main areas of concern for some service leavers is setting up a home. You may be looking to move out of service accommodation and into a rented or purchased property or you may already own your own home and looking to move. There is help available to anyone leaving the armed forces who needs to find somewhere to live. The joint service housing advice office (JSHAO) provides information and advice for service leavers and dependants who are about to return to civilian life. If you are a veteran currently in armed forces accommodation, they can help you to find a civilian home. The JSHAO can be contacted on: **07814 612120** or **www.gov. uk**. The following is taken from the JSHAO page on **www.gov.uk** website:

> "The JSHAO is the MOD's tri-service focal point to provide service personnel and their dependants with civilian housing information for those wishing to move to civilian accommodation at any time in their career, and for those during resettlement to assist with the transition to civilian life."

Housing policy in the UK is a devolved matter and there are significant variations in approach and policy across England, Scotland, Wales and

Northern Ireland. The responsibility for providing current and accurate housing advice to service leavers lies with the armed forces up to the point of discharge. This information is delivered by the Joint Service Housing Advice Office (JSHAO). Further information can be found within the Armed Forces Covenant (2011) which is now enshrined in British law and states that:

> In addressing the accommodation requirements of Service personnel, the MOD seeks to promote choice, recognising the benefits of stability and home ownership amongst members of the Armed forces where this is practicable and compatible with service requirements, and that their needs alter as they progress through the service and ultimately, return to civilian life. Where service personnel are entitled to publicly provided accommodation, it should be of good quality, affordable and suitably located. They should have priority status in applying for Government sponsored affordable housing schemes, and service leavers should retain this status for a period after discharge. Personnel may have access to tailored Armed forces housing schemes or financial arrangements, depending on their circumstances to help them in purchasing their own property. Those injured in service should also have preferential access to appropriate housing schemes as well as assistance with necessary adaptations to private housing or service accommodation whilst serving. Members of the Armed forces community should have the same access to social housing and other housing schemes as any other citizen, and not be disadvantaged in that respect by the requirement for mobility whilst in service.

The House of Commons library briefing paper of July 2016 quoted that: "Ex Service personnel do not automatically attract high priority for social housing. However, housing allocation schemes can provide for ex-service personnel to be afforded some additional priority when applying for social housing in most areas of the UK" (Ota and Wilson 2016). It is worth understanding your Local Authority's housing approach for veterans and when communicating with the Authorities, refer to the information in this chapter and other policy documents if necessary. You can get help to find somewhere to live from your local council. But each council will be different in the way it supports veterans and service leavers. The local council can give you free advice on housing options and advise if you are homeless or threatened with homelessness. Find your local council on the **www.gov.uk** website. It's worth remembering that there is legislation to help ensure fair treatment for armed forces personnel and veterans and that they are not disadvantaged by their service. The Armed Forces Bill enshrines the Armed Forces Covenant into law. You might find this a useful document: **https://www.gov.uk/government/news/new-legislastion-to-help-ensure-fair-treatment-for-armed-forces** if only to support any discussions you may have with local authorities. Don't be afraid to remind the local authorities of their commitment to the Armed Forces Covenant.

Other useful contacts are:

Haig Housing Trust – Haig Housing was formed in 2008 as a "sister charity" to Douglas Haig memorial homes. The aim of Haig Housing is to provide housing assistance to ex-service people and their dependants. The Trust also offers a range of housing advice to the service community and has more than 1,500 properties throughout the UK in over 50 different local authority regions. The properties are for rental only and are, in the main, suitable for families. You can contact Haig Housing Trust on: **www.haighousing.org.uk**

Alabare's Homes for Veterans provide supported accommodation to British armed forces veterans who are homeless or at risk of becoming homeless. Alabare's homes are provided across England and Wales, specifically, Devon, Dorset, Gloucestershire, Hampshire, Wiltshire, and North and South Wales. For more information contact: **www.alabare.co.uk or veterans@alabare.co.uk**

SSAFA – We mention SSAFA throughout the book, but the charity will support military veterans with housing issues. **www.ssafa.org.uk**

RENTING A HOME

If you have been occupying service accommodation for a period of time, you'd be forgiven for not understanding the detail of civilian tenancy agreements. Similarly, on Civvy Street there is housing legislation that must be followed, which is also something that you may not be familiar with. Understanding your rights and knowing about this legislation will help you and your family to settle into a new home.

Before signing any tenancy agreement, make sure your future landlord, or any letting agency, knows your requirements in terms of children, pets etc. Check that there are no restrictions for pets or smoking, as some landlords don't allow either. Make sure you fully understand your tenancy agreement before signing it, in terms of paying the rent and what to do if you know you are going to be late with payment. It is far better to tell the landlord or letting agent if you are going to be late with payment as you might be liable for extra fees. Landlords are increasingly asking for references from prospective tenants before they confirm the tenancy agreement, so you might want to secure a couple of referees from the military before leaving or have a couple of good contacts that can provide character or professional references for you. Some landlords require an amount of money as a deposit – to "hold" the property and many ask for one or two months' rent upfront. But your letting agent will be able to help you with this.

Make sure you are fully aware of who is responsible for paying bills such as utilities and council tax. If you are paying for utilities, shop around for the best supplier – you do not have to follow the landlord's suggestions. Before signing any tenancy agreement, make sure you check all the fixtures and fittings, and make notes and take photographs of any issues and report them to the landlord. Once you've signed the agreement, it's unlikely that you'll be able to get anything changed. Ask if you will be provided with an inventory of the property and fixture and fittings – it is not a legal requirement of the landlord but will help to avoid disputes. Check the agreement also for any sub-letting prohibitions. You might also want to be clear of the landlord's requirements in terms of any decorating you might want to carry out. You should get contents insurance for the things you own in the property as the landlord's insurance is not likely to cover these.

All rental properties must have at least one working smoke alarm per floor and if the property has a solid fuel or woodburning stove, it should be fitted with a carbon monoxide detector. If the property has gas, the landlord should provide you with a current gas safety certificate. From July 2020, the Electrical Safety Standards apply to all private rental properties. Landlords must provide a copy of the Electrical Safety condition report. Under the Homes Act (2018) the property must be safe, healthy, and free from things that could cause you serious harm, so check on your tenancy agreement whether you are exempt from paying rent if your property floods. Most letting agents will be pleased to guide you through this process, and there is plenty of information on agents' websites. We have used the website of Smith &Co (**www.smithandcoestates.co.uk**) simply as the front page sets out a clear step-by-step guide to considerations when renting or buying a property.

BUYING A HOME

The veterans' Gateway (**www.support.veteransgateway.org.uk**) offers help and guidance on purchasing a property in England, Scotland, Wales and Northern Ireland. But you first need to know how much you can afford. Banks and building societies offer mortgage loans and advice but there will be upfront costs, for example, deposits and surveys etc. Estate agents will guide you on this. The Veterans' Gateway suggests that you can apply for an interest-free loan through the forces' "help to buy" scheme whilst you are still serving – which could help with the cost of a deposit. There is more information on this on **www.gov.uk**. There are a variety of "help to buy" schemes in England which offer different ways to pay for your home. If you are currently serving, or if you are within two years of leaving, you have priority status for affordable homes. The charity "Shelter" can help with advice on this. **www.england.shelter.org.uk**

Usually, once you have decided what you can afford, you approach an estate agent to view the property several times before making the decision to buy. You might be dealing directly with the house builder if there is a "help to buy" scheme on a new housing development. You will have a set of criteria personal and unique to you when viewing a property, but some of the areas that will cost you a large amount of money if they are not maintained are: any wooden windows and door frames, windows and doors, the roof, and the damp course. Any survey you have done on the potential property should identify if there are any issues with these, but it's worth checking. There are advantages and disadvantages of buying a brand-new house, but one of the advantages is that it is likely to have a building warranty, so things like the roof, dampcourse and any other structural considerations should be covered for the life of the warranty. Also consider flood risk as your insurance might not cover flood damage if the house is built near a watercourse or flood plain. If there are several houses for sale in a small area, or on the same road, in the same terrace etc. it might indicate that there is a particular problem in that area, it might be a noise issue, so this might be worth checking out. Also consider neighbours: it might be worth visiting the property at night and weekend to get a feel for the neighbourhood. You might want to visit the immediate neighbours and inform them of your intent to purchase the property. The website **www. streetcheck.co.uk** is useful in giving in-depth information about property across the UK. You simply put in the postcode of the house and it offers information on the housing in the area, people, employment, culture, crime and other interesting facts about the vicinity.

Whether you are renting a home or buying a home, getting early and accurate advice and guidance is crucial, and it is always worth asking estate agents, mortgage lenders, rental agents and solicitors if they provide a distinct service for military veterans. It might be useful looking at rental services and estate agents which have signed the armed forces covenant as they are likely to be more sympathetic to your cause. Similarly, if you engage a solicitor to take care of your house purchase, you might want to choose one that has signed the armed forces covenant. But whoever you engage to support you in obtaining your new home, be assertive in your communication with them and know your rights prior to engaging with them. An estate agent wants to sell the house – they might not, therefore, be likely to tell you about the planning permission for the factory in the field next to the house that you are viewing, that it is up to you to find out. If you have a "search" completed along with a survey, this should identify any planning applications. But you can easily search this yourself by going on to the respective planning applications page of the local authority website. Most properties are put on the market for a price, knowing that the price will be reduced, so when you put an offer in, look if there are any other houses like the one you are considering for sale in that area and check out what they are on the market for. Your offer can then take this into consideration, but certainly think about putting an initial offer in that is lower than the asking price.

Finding a home is fundamental to your resettlement; whether you are renting or buying, the property will be where you begin your resettlement, so consider your options carefully and get advice as early as possible. If you have children, you will need to consider the schools in the area you are thinking of resettling to – the local authority website will have details of local schools. The individual school websites will also give you a good idea of how the school is managed and the sorts of activities the school offers. Many school websites identify the OFSTED rating for the school, though you might want to check this out on the OFSTED website yourself (**www.reports.ofsted.gov.uk**). You will be doing most of the chasing and administrative tasks yourself so be prepared to spend time following up with agents and solicitors.

SUMMARY

In this chapter we have provided some basic information and offered some signposts in terms of finding and either purchasing or renting a home. If you choose to rent via social housing or as it is sometimes referred to "going down the authority route", then your main contact will be the housing officer at your local authority housing department, who will be able to give you advice on bidding on social housing. Whether you choose to rent or buy, there will be a significant amount of paperwork to complete and check. This will be your responsibility, so don't file it where it's likely to get forgotten. Letting and selling agents and solicitors are usually rather good at helping in terms of what you need to complete and sign etc. but they may think you know all about it, about the process, so don't be frightened to tell them that you'll need help.

REFERENCES

Gutteridge, R. (2019) Ending Veteran Homelessness. *Pathfinder*. December 2019

Shiro Ota, Wilson, W. (2016) Housing options for serving and ex-military personnel. *Briefing paper.*

CHAPTER 4

FINANCE

INTRODUCTION

On leaving the Military, some people find themselves in financial difficulty. It is important if you are in this situation to get good advice and help at the earliest opportunity. The sooner money matters are being managed, the better, and the less chance there is of them getting out of control. It might sound obvious, but it is surprising how many people leave financial problems to fester, then it becomes more difficult to get on top of them and see a way to managing them. There are several agencies and organisations that can help you and offer advice; the money advice service is a good place to start **www.moneyadviceservice.org.uk** The thing to remember is, you won't be the first person with financial challenges that these services have helped, and you certainly won't be the last. They exist to offer help and support because there is a need for that type of advice, so use them. We mention this in more detail in the section on debt later in this chapter. We learnt from one of the veterans responding to the research that he had been given some bad advice (from a military colleague who had begun working for an investment company) regarding investing his pension into a scheme that turned out to be, let's just say, less than ethical. He, like many others, still doesn't know if he's lost all his pension. The message is, therefore, if you are tempted to invest your pension, or any other capital for that matter, get financial advice from an adviser that is trained, accredited and ideally a member of the Financial Conduct Authority (FCA).

PENSION

As you approach your Military service exit date, it may feel like you are being overloaded with advice, documents, and resettlement procedures. One of these documents will be your AFPS pens form 1. This will be sent to you either in your leavers pack or electronically. It is quite a long and detailed form, and some people find it quite a complex form to get your head around. However, it is an important document that you need to get right (Petley 2020). You might consider signing up to the Forces Pension Society (**https://forcespensionsociety.org** or tel: **020 7820 9988**. Email: **memsec@forpen.co.uk**). This organisation in a not-for-profit military pension watchdog acting on behalf of the entire military community. It offers a pension advisory service as well as regular communications keeping you informed of pension-related news, and provides access to expert pension advice. There are many other pension advice services that could be as helpful as the Forces Pension Society that are well worth a look, too. The Financial Conduct Authority (FCA) offers good general advice on pensions and the threats and scams that are sometimes used. The FCA website is full of useful information regarding pension scams and other pension advice **www.fca.org.uk** These are just a few of the pension advice services, but you may prefer to look out a pension adviser in your area, or a financial service or individual who has signed the Armed Forces Covenant.

- Financiable is a member of the Financial Conduct Authority and offers a free pension consultation. **www.financiable.co.uk**
- The Citizens Advice provides information on pension and compensations schemes for the armed forces, veterans, and their families. **www.citizensadvice.org.uk**
- My Pension Advisor connects you with a local FCA regulated

independent pension advisor, many offering free initial consultations. **www.mypensionadvisor.co.uk**

If you leave the military with a pension (either AFPS 75, AFPS 05 or early departure pension) and you are intending on engaging with further (military) service, you need to get advice on how your pensions will be affected by future salary and pension. Abatement rules apply in all cases, so our advice is that you seek guidance before committing to further service as your pay and pensions benefit in your new post cannot exceed your old rate of pay. Abatement rules only apply to future military employment and last only as long as that employment. If you go into future Civilian employment, it might also be worth seeking financial advice regarding your pensions as you will be taxed at the current rate on all your income (Petley 2020). If you are claiming a war pension or a war widows or widowers pension, Veterans UK (**0808 191 4218** or **veterans.help@spva.gsi.gov.uk**) can offer help, but if you join FPS, you can get tailored advice on this aspect of your pension income.

In terms of the State pension in the UK, before 6th April 2016 the state pension was made up of two parts: the basic state pension and the second state pension (SP2) which was designed to supplement the basic state pension. All national insurance contributions counted towards the basic state pension. A lot of employers' pension schemes (including the Armed Forces Pension scheme) contracted out of the SP2. This meant that all members of the scheme paid 1.4% less national insurance. However, it also meant that members received a smaller overall state pension. From April 2016, this changed and everyone in the UK who pays class 1 national insurance contributions pays the contributions at the same higher rate. So, everyone who joined the military before 2016 is likely to have a combination pension of both contribution schemes. The old basic state pension rate (from 6th April 2019) is £129.20 per week. The newer single rate pension from the same date is £168.60 per week. The information above was taken from The Pathfinder (Petley 2019: page 6). It is a good idea to check your contribution record and there are several ways of doing this. Currently, you can contact the national insurance contributions office (from UK – tel:

0345 3000 169, from outside UK – tel: **0345 3000 168**, or you can check on-line at: **https://www.tax.service.gov.uk/check-your-state-pension**)

WELFARE AND BENEFITS

There are a wide range of benefits that may be accessible to you, having served in the armed forces; these include: Child benefit, statutory sick pay, housing benefit, working and child tax credits, armed forces independent payment, personal independent payment, attendance allowance, job-seekers allowance, and tax credits. You may also be entitled to: Council tax relief, help with school fees for children, help with childcare costs, and free or reduced travel costs. Citizens Advice is a good place to start for unbiased and non-judgemental advice if you are inquiring about any of these benefits (**www.citizensadvice.org.uk**). **It is really important that you claim all the help that you are entitled to.** According to **www. MoneySavingExpert.com** over £10 billion of benefits were left unclaimed in 2018. No one is likely to tell you that you are entitled to these, it's up to you to check it out, but it's worth finding out if you are entitled to any benefits, either financial, or in the way of credits.

If you have an injury, illness, or disablement (physical or mental) either because of your service, or that has occurred since you left the military, you may be entitled to Personal Independent Payment or Attendance Allowance. You may be able to claim for these even if your needs were not because of your military service. Many civilians claim for these benefits because of non-occupational illness. **We encourage you to apply for these benefits** as we discuss in the chapter on Health and Wellbeing. The Royal British Legion (**www.britishlegion.org.uk**) and SSAFA (**www.ssafa.org. uk**) can help you to apply for these benefits. But as we have already said, you will probably need to drive the communications with these charities, and be clear and assertive when doing so.

There are various travel schemes for Veterans. For some schemes, various conditions apply, but it is worth finding out what the schemes are and what you are entitled to. You can apply for the Veterans Concessionary travel scheme in London if you are already getting financial help – Transport for London can help you with this (**0845 331 9872** or **www.tfl.gov.uk**). In Scotland, the National Entitlement Card allows free bus travel anywhere in Scotland for injured veterans; the information on how to apply for the card is available from Travel Scotland (**0141 272 7100**. Or **www.transport.gov.scot**). In Wales, some seriously injured service personnel are entitled to free bus travel anywhere in Wales; information for this is at **www.wales.gov.uk**.

Armed forces personnel, husbands, wives, and children can buy the Forces Railcard. This gives a third off most rail fares throughout the UK in any given year. You can find out more about this scheme at: **www.hmforces-railcard.co.uk**

Service leavers and military veterans can access other discounts for many goods and services – the best place to find out about this is: **www.defencediscountservice.co.uk**. These discounts are available both on-line and on the high street by using the Defence Privilege Card. As an example (and this list is by no means exhaustive) the following companies accept the Defence Privilege card:

Samsung, Starbucks, BT, GO Outdoors, Halfords, KFC, O2, Ray Ban, Vue, Apple, Cineworld, Hotpoint and ODEON.

DEBT ADVICE

If you are struggling with debt, the earliest you seek support and advice, the better. It can be really hard to know where to turn and the longer you leave it before getting help, the more worrying you will do, which will not help you to address your debt issues. It is worth getting specialist advice on debt as the people giving this advice are trained and experienced professionals who are used to supporting people to regain control of their finances. A good place to start is the Money Advice Service at **www.moneyadviceservice.org.uk** This is a free, confidential service that offers either on-line debt advice, telephone advice, or face-to-face advice. The advisers working at the service never make judgement on any individuals seeking advice, nor do they make you feel bad about your situation. They're listening to people with debt problems every day, so are used to and experienced in helping people to manage debt. They will always be willing and happy to listen to your debt issues, no matter how big or how small, and they will help you to find ways of managing your money, even if you think there are no alternatives. But most importantly they are the specialists who may be able to suggest ways to deal with debts that you might not know about. The website also allows you to search for a debt advisor in your area if you prefer face-to-face or a more personal conversation.

There are other debt charities that have successfully helped people to come to terms with debt and to get their finances in order, and we list some here, but this is by no means the extent of organisations that support people with debt.

StepChange Debt Charity: **www.stepchange.org**. Tel: **0800 138 1111**

Debt Advice Foundation: **www.debtadvicefoundation.org**. Tel: **0800 622 6151**

National Debtline: **www.tools.nationaldebtline.org/dat-reg**. Tel: **0808 808 4000**

Citizens Advice: **www.citizensadvice.org.uk**

FINANCIAL ASSISTANCE AND LOANS

The publication "Financial and money advice for veterans" (MOD and Veterans UK 2020) is worth reading as it gives advice on veteran-focused money, debt advice and information on the different types of financial support available via the Veterans' Gateway. For financial loans, your bank may well be the first place to start in finding out how much you can loan and the repayment details. There are many money lenders waiting to lend you any amount of cash, but you should exercise caution as many of these have exceptionally large interest payments attached. Also be careful before taking out a Payday loan. These loans are short term unsecured loans that are often characterised by extremely high interest rates. These loans are also called cash advances. A study by Gathergood et al (2019) found that payday loans cause significant increase in defaults and cause many consumers to exceed their bank overdraft limits. Basically, these loans involve a lender providing a short-term unsecured loan to be repaid at the next borrower's pay day. It is sometimes very easy to apply for and get these loans via an on-line application. Sadly, austerity, low wages, and insecure work drive people to take on high-cost payday loans, some from lenders who are ripping off the borrowers. We suggest that you get specialist advice before taking out any loan.

Unless you are a financial expert, there is something to be said for getting expert and specialist advice at the earliest opportunity if you require guidance on any aspect of your finances. These financial services and advisors know the financial landscape and will be able to offer advice that is personal to you and your situation. There may be independent financial advisers that have signed the armed forces covenant and so may be familiar with the sorts of financial advice you require; it would certainly be worth checking out which financial consultants and advisers have done this.

SUMMARY

When you leave the military, it is understandable that you feel exposed and vulnerable, as we've said. But your finances need to be protected. Make sure you know exactly where your money is – for example, your pension and any other capital that you might have. We've discussed what can happen if you entrust someone to your pension – just because you know them and they've also been in the military doesn't necessarily mean they'll look after your money. We cannot emphasise enough that you should act on finance advice that has been given to you from a qualified and accredited financial advisor. Don't be tempted to trust someone with your money because they seem like a decent person. It is not uncommon to hear of people being duped out of life savings and pensions because the alleged financial advice was given by seemingly well-meaning people.

REFERENCES

Gathergood, J. Guttman-Kenney, B. and Hunt, S (2019) How do payday loans affect borrowers? Evidence from the UK Market. *Review of Financial Studies* 32 (2).

MoneySavingExpert.com – www.MoneySavingExpert.com

Petley, M (2020) Getting the PENS form 1 right. *Pathfinder* (May 2020: 6)

Petley, M. (2019) The State Pension – just a little reminder. *Pathfinder* (December 2019)

CHAPTER 5

HEALTH AND WELL-BEING

INTRODUCTION

Physical and mental health challenges for service leavers and veterans are well documented. It is difficult to comprehend that service personnel who are prepared to give their lives for the Country are amongst those at greater risk of mental ill health when returning to civilian life after serving in the military. We don't attempt to go into any detail of illnesses or conditions in this book, but rather, this chapter is intended to offer some guidance and signposting to some of the health and well-being services that are available for people transitioning to civilian life. There are some actions that we suggest you address, but in the main, we provide some of the opportunities for support that are accessible to you. These are by no means the only organisations or charities that are available for support; there are many more. You might find looking through these helps you to understand what help is available, but there is no real substitute for you to research the help that is available that supports your own personal issues.

Once you transition from the military to civilian life in the UK your healthcare services are supplied by the NHS. **Therefore, the first action you should take after leaving the military is to register with an NHS**

medial practice/ General practitioner and present your military medical record summary. This is also an opportunity to discuss your health with the GP and ensure that any concerns are documented on your records. If you are not sure which medical practice or GP to contact, the NHS has a GP finder service, where you simply put in your postcode and press search for your nearest NHS medical practice – you can find this on **www.nhs.uk** and search for "find a GP". In England, subject to the clinical needs of others, military veterans are entitled to priority NHS treatment for any condition (physical or mental) that may have been caused by their service in the military (NHS 2020). Legislation has been passed in January 2021 to help to ensure that armed forces personnel and their families are not disadvantaged by their service when accessing key public services (MOD 2021). In enshrining the Armed Forces Bill into law, the legislation will embed the Armed Forces Covenant, which will require all relevant UK public bodies to have due regard to the principles of the covenant. This is a positive move as research by the Mental Health Foundation found that ex-service personnel are vulnerable to several risk factors including social exclusion and homelessness, each posing risk factors for mental ill health. Other research has found that experiences both during service and through transition to civilian life means that mental ill health may also be triggered by other factors; these include and are not limited to: substance abuse, depression, anxiety, stress and a sense of loss (Fear et al 2010). The sad finding in all this is that only half of those with mental health problems seek help from the NHS after leaving the military for reasons including:

- Trying to manage alone (or with family)
- Fear of criticism or ridicule
- Embarrassment
- Think that the NHS won't understand. (NHS 2021)

We cannot stress the importance of getting help and getting it as early as possible. The professionals working in the mental health services in the NHS specialise in helping people with all or any of the above concerns and will understand any emotional or mental health issues that are presented to them.

CAREER TRANSITION PARTNERSHIP (CTP)

Although this book is focused on your life once you have left the military, it seems logical to address support programmes that span the transition period. We have already mentioned the CTP, and you'll no doubt have accessed the support it offers in some form or other. The "CTP Assist" is charged with supporting service leavers who are being, or who are likely to be, medically discharged and who have been deemed to require additional support regardless of length of service. Medical discharge service leavers may need longer in resettlement and access to specialist services; it is also possible to defer resettlement for up to two years after discharge for those not able to undertake routine resettlement due to their medical condition (MOD 2015).

RESETTLEMENT AND MANAGING MENTAL HEALTH TRANSITION TO CIVILIAN LIFE

Most service leavers apparently go through resettlement and enter civilian life without experiencing any mental health issues. The Mental Health Foundation has suggested that 0.5% of ex-service personnel have mental ill health when they enter Civvy Street (MHF 2020). But our question is: how does the Foundation know if, as the NHS has reported, only half may present to a GP or mental health service? So, there could be many more service leavers and veterans with mental ill health than is fully recognised. Maybe this is the reason that some develop quite serious mental ill health after leaving the service. There is strong evidence to suggest that seeking help as early as possible is beneficial (Mind 2017). Getting help is the first step to getting better and staying well, but it is often difficult to know where to start or who to turn to, and it is the individuals themselves who normally must make the first move to seek support. It is this point that we would like to stress. From the conversations we have had with veterans regarding their resettlement and particularly those who have mental health needs, it seems that the first request for help from the individual themselves is the most difficult. But we argue that this is the most important. There is absolutely no shame or embarrassment, or any other negative feeling to be worried about in seeking help for emotional or mental health issues. Feeling a loss of control or being out of your depth are not uncommon as seeking well-being support is something that you have probably never had to do before. It's also understandable that you might want to try to sort things out for yourself or on your own. But, if this is you, ask yourself this: Are you a mental health specialist? Do you understand the complex workings of the mind? If not, then you might benefit from talking to someone who is. **We advocate for seeking help at the earliest opportunity** and if you don't feel able to contact your GP for whatever reason, then we suggest you contact one of the services listed here in this book. You might think that you are not too bad, that you are not somehow "ill enough" to seek help. Mind (2017) has reported that people ask for help if they're:

- Worrying about things more than usual
- Finding it hard to enjoy life and feel happy
- Having thoughts and feelings that are difficult to cope with and negatively impacting on daily life.

Specialist intervention at this stage can often prevent any mental ill health from getting worse. Please talk to someone, anyone, if you or any other service leavers or veterans you know are experiencing any sort of emotional or mental health challenges.

It is worth reflecting on the fact that your military training and experience created a sense of belonging and team spirit, of strong camaraderie and discipline, all of which are probably missing during the early stages of resettlement. So, it's no wonder then that some service leavers suffer with emotional and mental problems when leaving the military. Civvy Street is sometimes a tricky place to negotiate for people who have lived in it for years, so for someone fresh out of the services, it's only to be expected that you may experience some struggles. Not least because things on the Street change so rapidly and if you have been unable to keep up with the changes, it'll probably feel like a different world. It's good to know then that there are numerous organisations and services that are available and accessible to service leavers and veterans. We discuss some here, but these are by no means the extent of services available to you. The NHS is perhaps the best place to get information if you are unsure which service to approach.

From the perspective of those civilians who are in positions of being able to support military veterans and those going through resettlement, Dr Jonathan Leach (ex RAMC) advises that using the right language is "hugely important when talking through mental health issues with veterans" (Leach 2020: 22). He argues that the medicine on Civvy Street is the same, it's the experiences of those taking it that is different, and it is these experiences that require a different approach in terms of communication and interaction. This presents something of a challenge as the military language and "banter" can sometimes be misinterpreted on Civvy Street. Similarly, the language used on Civvy Street might appear strange to those who have been in military service. One of the veterans we spoke to for the research for this book talked of "needing a Civvy phrase book" specifically regarding job applications and employment on Civvy Street.

The mental health of military leavers and veterans has been the subject of much debate. The Ministry of Defence and the NHS now work together in partnership to provide physical and mental health support for people going through resettlement. The following services have been developed specifically for ex-military personnel and so have specialist practitioners working for them who have a knowledge and understanding of the types of conditions that are likely to be presented. All conversations with each of these services are confidential and handled sensitively and compassionately.

VETERANS' MENTAL HEALTH TRANSITION INTERVENTION AND LIAISON SERVICE (TILS)

This is the **first point of contact** for anyone who has a discharge date, is transitioning out of the service and who needs support for their emotional or mental health. This service provides a specialised assessment that will determine what sort of support and/or treatment needs to be considered. The assessments are carried out by expert staff with a knowledge and understanding of military veterans' needs. The service staff are keen to hear from any veterans or reserves who feel they may need emotional or mental health support, or if they have been advised to get help from family members.

For England:

North of England: Tel: **0303 123 1145** email: **www.veteransservicelse.nhs.uk**

Midlands and East of England: Tel: **0300 323 0137** email: **mevs.mhm@nhs.net**

London and South East England: Tel: **020 3317 6818** email: **cim-tr.veteranstilservice-lse@nhs.net**

South West of England: Tel: **0300 365 2000** email: **gateway@berkshire.nhs.uk**

For Scotland:

Veterans First Point Scotland is an NHS partnership with a network of six regional centres across Scotland providing support to veterans. It provides a veteran-led mental health and welfare support service. This is best accessed by the website: **www.veteransfirstpoint.org.uk**

For Wales:

Veterans Wales is an NHS service for veterans in need of mental health support in Wales. Veterans can refer themselves for access to an experienced veteran therapist. Each local health board in Wales has an experienced Veteran Therapist (VT). They accept referrals from healthcare staff, GPs, veterans' charities and self-referrals. The website: **www.veteranswales. co.uk** is the best source of information and contacts. The telephone number is: **029 2183 2261**

For Northern Ireland:

AA Veterans Support was established in 2011 to provide help, advice and guidance including mental health support to those who serve or who have served in the British forces and their families throughout Northern Ireland. AAVS can also signpost to other specialist health services for veterans in Northern Ireland. The website **www.aavsni.com** has more information and contact details. The telephone number is: **028 9074 7071**.

VETERANS' MENTAL HEALTH COMPLEX TREATMENT SERVICE (CTS)

This service is for military veterans who have service-related complex mental health problems that have not improved with earlier intervention. This could be including but not limited to: substance misuse, substance addiction, other addictions, physical health needs, housing problems and financial problems. Again, this service is operated by experts in the field of supporting ex-military personnel. CTS is accessed via TILS or other referral agencies and services.

VETERANS' MENTAL HEALTH HIGH INTENSITY SERVICE (HIS)

This service provides focused intensive care and treatment to veterans and service leavers presenting with significant mental health problems. It is run by expert practitioners with a vast experience of the Military.

THE VETERANS AND RESERVES MENTAL HEALTH PROGRAMME (VRMHP)

The VRMHP is formerly the Medical Assessment Programme. It provides mental health assessment for veterans and reserves who have concerns about their mental health.

Many articles have been written and research projects undertaken on specific conditions and mental illnesses. We do not address these in detail in this book, but Post Traumatic Stress Disorder in military personnel is well documented and so we do offer some brief discussion on this condition, but much more information on PTSD in military veterans can be accessed from PTSD UK. According to PTSD UK (2021), PTSD is a significant concern amongst military personnel and veterans, so anything we can do to encourage people to seek help is important. We have therefore mentioned some considerations around PTSD in the following paragraph and signposted to organisations that provide focused information and support for people experiencing PTSD.

POST-TRAUMATIC STRESS DISORDER (PTSD)

PTSD is caused by being exposed to or witnessing a traumatic event. "The defining characteristic of PTSD is its capacity to provoke fear, helplessness, or horror in response to the threat of injury or death and can therefore affect anyone" (PTSDUK 2021). There are several examples of PTSD, and military service and combat is a key one of these. Military personnel experience events and pressures that most civilians can't begin to imagine; this leaves them extremely vulnerable to the debilitating effects of PTSD or *combat stress* as it is sometimes called. Armed forces personnel are often physically and mentally stretched for long periods of time, carrying out tasks in often horrific circumstances. For some this level and degree of stress is incapacitating. It's no wonder then, that PTSD is so common in service personnel and in military veterans. It's a great shame then that so many of these men and women consider it a taboo to ask for help or support. Organisations and support services that are concerned with PTSD are continually working out ways of encouraging veterans to seek help. PTSD UK – the only charity in the UK dedicated to raising awareness of the condition has a useful website with information – **www.ptsduk.org** Similarly, Combat Stress, the UK leading charity for veterans' mental health supports veterans and families on all areas of mental health. The charity has a 24-hour helpline **0800 138 1619** for veterans and families for confidential mental health advice and support. Help can also be accessed via the website on **www.combatstress.org.uk** SSAFA is another charitable organisation that supports military personnel transitioning to Civvy Street and has a dedicated mental health section; SSAFA can be contacted at **www.ssafa.org.uk** or on telephone: **0800 731 4880**. (SSAFA will also help in your search for a General Practitioner of medical centre if you are unable to do so yourself.)

It is also worth considering a comparative view. Based on research carried out in 2014, PTSD rates are perhaps surprisingly low amongst the British forces with rates of around 4% in personnel who have deployed to 6% in combat troops (Hunt et al 2014). This would seem to contradict some of what is reported in the media and much of what was the impression of the individuals that formed the case studies for this book.

ALCOHOL DEPENDENCY

Excessive alcohol consumption is not unusual in the armed forces. Sharing a drink is often thought an appropriate way to boost morale and comradeship and is not necessarily a negative thing. However, alcohol is very addictive for some people, and the line between moderate consumption and excessiveness is blurred in some cases. "Excessive alcohol use is more common in the armed forces and amongst veterans than in the civilian population. The fact that heavier drinking patterns established whilst serving often continue after leaving the forces, is a particular worry" (Misell 2020:2). A useful document regarding alcohol problems on service personnel and veterans is available at: **https://s31949.pcdn.c0/wp-content/upload** It is "Help-seeking for alcohol problems in serving and ex-serving UK military personnel" (Gribble, R., Stevelink, S. Goodwinn, L. and Fear, N. 2020). The report found that the recognition of alcohol problems and misuse in people seeking help for this in UK military veterans is low. The report offered several recommendations, which include:

- Conversations about alcohol within the military should be changed
- Alcohol intervention programmes should be available to all
- Increased support for personnel and families affected by alcohol issues
- Better access to available treatments
- Alcohol and mental health treatments need to be aligned

If you struggle with alcohol problems, then your GP will be able to advise you of treatments or services that are available to you. Medical practitioners are no strangers to supporting people to get help with alcohol dependency and addiction. The earlier you get help, the better. You can also contact Alcoholics Anonymous on **0800 9177 650** or at **www.alcohollics-anonymous.org.uk** and at **help@aamail.org**

GAMBLING

Gambling addiction is an impulsive-control disorder, if you are a compulsive gambler, you are unlikely to be able to control the urge and impulse to gamble, even when it has negative consequences for you and your loved ones. Being a compulsive gambler can lead to other health problems and relationship difficulties and leave you in serious debt. There is good evidence to suggest that a gambling addiction can be successfully treated in a similar way to other addictions. The best results are usually from Cognitive Behaviour Therapy (NHS 2021) and you can get access to this from your GP. There are other organisations that can help with gambling:

GamCare offers free information and counselling support for problem gamblers on **0808 8020 133**.

Gamblers Anonymous UK on **www.gamblersanonymous.org.uk** or **info@gamblersanonymous.org.uk**

As with other addictions, there is no shame in getting help and the sooner you access help, the better for you and for your family and friends.

IMPACT OF CORONAVIRUS ON MENTAL HEALTH

The global pandemic has impacted on all of society, so for those people with mental or emotional issues it could be particularly severe. People for whom socialisation is important will be particularly vulnerable to the pandemic restrictions and lockdown regulations and for those who need to travel and meet therapists etc, the lockdown could create significant challenges. In Pathfinder magazine July 2020 (Pathfinder 2020: 5) it was reported that a study to understand the impact that the Coronavirus has on military veterans will be carried out by the King's Centre for military health research at King's College London. The study will focus on whether the Covid-19 pandemic has had any significant impact on the Veteran community in the UK. This research report will be available at **www.kcl.ac.uk/kcmhr** once it is completed (likely to be Autumn 2021). John Owens, an ambassador for the Help for Heroes charity wrote in the Pathfinder April 2020 that the Coronavirus has left lots of people feeling anxious and as a result, the charity has created an on-line toolkit for military families who are struggling to adapt to a new way of living (**www.helpforheroes.org.uk**).

MENTAL HEALTH AND SOCIAL MEDIA

We live in a world that is increasingly connected by virtual means as is evidenced by the vast array of social media platforms available to us at the click of a button from a hand-held device that is often a constant companion. This has created a level of connectivity that is easy to take for granted and difficult to distance ourselves from. Apps such as Facebook, LinkedIn, YouTube etc. consume much of our lives with constant information and live news that display all sorts of views, opinions, and images, some of which are useful and helpful, and indeed, enable some of the more isolated and vulnerable people to feel a sense of belonging (to a virtual group etc). However, there is a less pleasant side to this form of communication as some sites and groups exploit the more vulnerable by "trolling" information and posting negative comments and, sometimes, extreme unpleasantness and hate. The concern is that in the quest to find "like minded" individuals and groups for support and interaction, the tendency is to get drawn in to the very plausible and enticing stuff that is promoted by trolls and other damaging unpleasantness. Confidence Tricksters are rife on social media; they are people who spend their time searching the internet for vulnerable or generally unassuming people to vent their poison and toxic spleen virtually, where they can't be identified or found. This isn't helpful for anyone suffering with emotional or mental health issues, as to be targeted by a troll can be traumatic and, sadly, as has been reported in the media, sometimes fatal. It is important then that we understand and use social media carefully and with caution. Never post any personal details, and certainly not your financial or private and confidential credentials. Once your information is out there in the virtual "ether" it is almost impossible to retrieve it and be 100% sure someone has not hit on it. We suggest a set of social media do's and don'ts, that might prevent activity from adding to existing, or creating new, mental, or emotional health struggles:

- Don't think everything you read on social media is the truth
- Don't think everything you read is for your benefit

- Don't think you have to respond to posts
- Don't take anything too seriously
- Don't be tempted to post anything that might be interpreted as hate
- Don't give any personal or private information on any platform
- Do look for genuine sites and groups that are validated in some way
- Do protect all your passwords and store then securely
- Do remember that your friends' accounts can be hacked and so mail may seem like it's coming from them when it isn't
- Do use social media to network and communicate carefully and responsibly.

MEDICAL DISCHARGE

In England, Wales and Northern Ireland, medical discharge procedures vary depending on the type of military service you have completed. You may have been through a medical board if you've been injured or sick during your service to have your medical grading assessed. This may or may not lead to medical discharge. This board assesses the physical and mental capacities and makes recommendations regarding discharge. The final decision regarding discharge is made by an occupational health specialist. Depending on the length of service and severity of your injuries, as well as your pension scheme, you may be entitled to receive terminal benefits. This benefit is paid upon discharge (**https://support.veteransgateway. org.uk**/). More information regarding this is available from the Joint Personnel Enquiry Centre on **0800 085 3600**. If it was your service that led to your illness or injury, you may be entitled to a War Pension (if the injury occurred prior to April 2005) or Armed forces compensation (if the injury was after the 6TH April 2005). For more information on this, please contact Veterans UK. The Royal British Legion can also help and offer advice regarding medical discharge (**www.britishlegion.org.uk**). SSAFA are also able to assist and refer you to specialists for advice concerning military discharge (**www.ssafa.org.uk**).

GETTING HELP FOR ILLNESS AND INJURY ON CIVVY STREET

In England and Wales you may be entitled to get a Personal Independent Payment (PIP). This benefit replaces the disability living allowance and is for people aged 16–64 with a long-term mental or physical illness or disability. If you do have a long-term condition, it is worth finding out if you are able to get a PIP payment. You will need to complete an application form and undergo an assessment, but the PIP advice and advocacy service can help you to do this (tel: **0800 917 2222** or **www.contact.org.uk** In Scotland, the site: **www.veteransscotland.co.uk** has information on the support that is available for military veterans north of the border. In Wales, the veteran population with an injury or illness attributable to their military service can access information regarding the support that is available on: **www2. nphs.wales.nhs.uk** For injured veterans in Northern Ireland, the Forces in Mind Trust has accessible information regarding support that is available: **www.fim-trust.org**

For those over 65 years of age in England, Wales and Northern Ireland, you may be entitled to an Attendance Allowance. This is a non-means tested benefit to support people who have mental or physical disability or care needs. The benefit is paid at two different rates depending on the level of care required. The Department of Work and Pensions is a good source of information regarding this benefit (**www.gov.uk**). If you receive a War disablement pension, you may also be entitled to get a Constant Attendance Allowance.

We suggest that if you have any illness because of your service, no matter how minor you feel this is, that you either contact your GP to begin your application for a benefit or that you contact one of the organisations above. You are absolutely entitled to apply for these benefits.

JOINING CIVVY STREET WITH PHYSICAL INJURIES

The Veterans Trauma Network provides care and treatment to those who have sustained injuries because of their military service. The network is available in selected NHS health centres across England. Veterans who access the service that this network provides, will be cared for by professionals who understand the nature of the injuries. The Veterans Trauma Network works closely with The Defence Medical Services, NHS Veterans mental health services and certain Military charities. The network ensures that all patients have a personalised plan of care in place. The network supports families as well as the injured veteran, which is particularly useful for accessing services that may be able to provide support. If you need help yourself from the network or know someone who does, the referral process is straightforward. Firstly, register with an NHS GP (informing them that you have served in the armed forces), if you have not already done so. Then you need to inform your GP that you would like them to refer you to the network – they can do this by emailing: **England. veteranstraumanetwork@nhs.net** or you can contact Blesma (see below)

> **Blesma** – Assist limbless and injured veterans to lead independent and fulfilling lives after life changing injuries. Dedicated to supporting both serving and ex-service men and women who have suffered limb loss or the loss of use of a limb, eye or loss of sight. Blesma assists by providing support networks where members can access support from a professional Blesma welfare team that can offer support in terms of getting grants and advice with allowance claims, but probably the biggest benefit to belonging to an organisation such as Blesma is the sense of belonging. Blesma is a network community of like-minded people who have similar injuries. The charity prides itself on being an association founded on a strong sense of camaraderie and providing practical support on things such as finance and housing.

Contact Blesma on: Tel. **020 8548 7080** or email: **membersupport@ blesma.org**

Getting early and appropriate help is the best move you can make if you think you may need support when leaving the military and beginning your life on Civvy Street. If you don't feel able to make that first call, ask someone else to on your behalf; they will be able to get so far, but then, as your condition is private and confidential to you, you'll have to engage with the respective professionals or organisations as soon as you feel able.

SUMMARY

The NHS is arguably one of this Country's success stories. Once you leave the military your health will be the concern of the NHS so as we've said, you must register with a medical practitioner as soon as possible and inform them of your military service and medical record. We don't make any excuses for repeating our appeal that you seek help at the earliest opportunity for any physical or mental health issue that you may have. The medical professionals that you deal with are trained and experienced people who are employed to ensure people like you get the help you need and deserve. There are stories in the media of times that the NHS has allegedly failed people, but sadly, all the success stories and times when people's health has been saved and improved don't attract the same media attention. We have included in this chapter some relevant signposts, but there will be many more that will be distinct to your area, so do make yourself familiar with NHS services available to you near to where you live.

REFERENCES

Fear, N., Jones, M. and Murphy, D. (2010) What are the consequences of deployment to Iraq and Afghanistan on the mental health of the armed forces? A cohort study. *The Lancet.* 375 (9728) 1783 – 1797

Gribble, R., Spanakis, P., Stevelink, S.,Rona, R., Fear, N. and Goodwin, L. (2020) *Help seeking for alcohol problems in serving and ex-serving UK military personnel.* A joint report by the King's Centre for Military Health Research and The University of Liverpool.

Hunt, E., Wessley, S., Jones, N., Rona, R. and Greenberg, N. (2014) The mental health of the UK Armed forces: where fact meets fiction. *European Journal of Psychotraumatology*. On www.kcl.ac.uk

Leach, J. (2020) Good communication is at the heart of my approach. *Soldier*. March 2020.

Mental Health Foundation (2021) Mental health foundation on www.mentalhealth. org.uk

Mind (2017) Seeking help for a mental health problem. www.mind.org.uk

Ministry of Defence (2015) Information for Service leavers. Updated October 2015 www.gov.uk

Ministry of Defence (2021) Armed Forces Bill. MOD. January 2021. www.gov.uk

NHS (2020) Veterans: NHS mental health services. www.nhs.uk

PTSD UK (2021) Causes of PTSD. www.ptsduk.org

Signpost

Beyond the Battlefield – A charity that is concerned with the well-being of veterans in both parts of the island of Ireland. The charity focuses on PTSD and supports all service personnel, both police and the emergency services as well as the armed forces.

SSAFA – Has branches in England, Wales, Scotland and Northern Ireland. To find your local branch, contact **www.ssafa.org.uk**

Dedicated Health Services for ex-forces (PDF 278KB) **www.assets.nhs.uk** For information regarding health services and NHS dedicated services.

CHAPTER 6

LEARNING AND TRANSFERABLE SKILLS

INTRODUCTION

Whilst you were serving in the military you may have been aware of the Armed Forces Learning Credits Scheme which was intended to support your personal and professional development. There are two types of credits: Standard Learning Credits (SLCs) which fund small learning events and Enhanced Learning Credits (ELCs) which fund or help to fund further and higher education courses and qualifications. These credits can be accessed up to five years after your date of discharge. Some service leavers with eligible service (see JSP8220) will be able to access the credits up to 10 years from discharge. The credits can be combined with the Individual Resettlement Training Cost (IRTC) grant to pay the cost of tuition fees. However, if you use the ELCs your course must lead to a nationally recognised qualification at Level 3 or above.

This chapter will focus on using some of the skills, knowledge and understanding you have already built up to support your future personal and professional development on Civvy Street. We go into a bit more detail in terms of transferring these skills and how you might save yourself time in any future training you might decide to do.

After speaking with several people who have recently left the military and who have embarked on university courses, we are able to draw on some useful insights that might be relevant to anyone considering embarking on further training or academic qualifications.

PERSONAL AND TRANSFERABLE SKILLS

Our research prior to compiling this handbook identified that there is a sense that what you did in the military needs to stay in the military, and where there will obviously be situations that you would not be able to reconstruct or repeat situations and events, there will be plenty of opportunity to use many of the military skills to your benefit. Transferability applies to the transfer of skills from experiences in both work and in learning. We consider each of these learning situations and offer some suggestions as to how you can transfer your "military" skills into "civilian" skills. Some of the veterans we spoke to told us that it was the military that "made" them. They felt that they are who they are because of the training and experiences they had whilst serving, so it's no surprise that some find it challenging to resettle into civilian life. This chapter offers you the opportunity to reflect on your personal skills and preferences, and to identify how you can enhance these to support your transition. We look at what learning is, and you are encouraged to consider the notion of learning, and in doing so, reflect on how adults learn. Some learning theory is introduced to the discussion to offer an explanation and argument for different learning methods, but we do not dwell too much on the theoretical nature of learning. We offer the opportunity for you to discover your own preferred learning style by taking a learning styles questionnaire. In discovering how you might learn best, you are giving yourself a good base for any future opportunities.

A transferable skill is one which can be used in different roles or occupations. Skills and attributes such as: problem solving, leadership, coaching, team working, motivation and communications are just a few of the skills you are likely to have developed successfully whilst serving in the military. We will analyse these and other transferable skills you are likely to have built up and in doing so, we will look at how these skills can be used in civilian contexts.

> "There are certain keywords in almost every job posting that relate to skills: Communication, multitasking, teamwork, creativity, critical thinking and leadership. These words represent a secret language that few job hunters understand. The ones that do "get it" are also the ones that get the job offers. That's because these keywords and phrases represent the skills that enable you to do your job well, whatever that job may be. They are known as Transferable skills because, no matter what the job or profession is, they make the difference between success and failure" (Yate 2017).

We have selected a few of the main skills that the veterans in our research alluded to as being the key skills they felt mattered most when they embarked on further training. As you read the following analysis of each of these transferable skills, consider how they have featured in your past work life, and think about your strengths and weaknesses associated for each of the skills. For example, you might reflect on a particular set of circumstances in which you led a team to complete a challenging project. You may recall specific instances and be able to identify how you performed successfully on certain aspects of leadership, but that you were less successful at others. Whenever you reflect on a transferable skill that requires some element of improvement, you have discovered a professional development opportunity to improve that skill. Reflecting on these occasions may be difficult for some, as the experiences you have had could offer some painful memories, but if you are able to recall some experiences and reflect on them with an objective view, you will become more confident in your skills and knowledge, and this will give you confidence when applying for education or training courses and completing job applications and in interviews.

CONFIDENCE

Having confidence and being confident in yourself can help massively in being successful in whatever you choose to do. But to display confidence appropriately, without portraying yourself as over-confident or arrogant, you also need to develop or make the most of your competence. Having a sense of self-confidence might enable you to seek advice from others, it might even underpin your ability to stand in front of a conference hall and present a seminar, but it's having the knowledge and humility and being able to develop your skills from learning that will ultimately lead to your success. This can't happen overnight, it takes time. Time to learn and develop your knowledge and understanding of something, or time to learn and develop a skill.

> If competence is the bricks then confidence is the mortar. You need both to build both a successful house and a successful life.
>
> McGee (2020)

But what is confidence?

There are a few definitions of confidence and plenty of gurus who claim to be able to make you a more 'confident' person, but what do we mean by being confident? Or having self-confidence? Academics and researchers don't necessarily agree on a definitive notion of confidence. Some consider it to have the ability to believe in yourself, others talk about it being something to do with knowing who and where you are in life, and what expectations you have. We argue that confidence is about trusting in your own abilities and believing you can do what you set out to do. But the caveat we place on this is, to display an appropriate level of confidence you also need to be able to acknowledge your own limitations and weaknesses. In drawing on the work of Parker et al (2014), we call this the *confidence balance*. Some of the most confident people are the first to ask for help or to admit to needing advice and guidance. Developing self-confidence effectively is usually progressive. You gradually build it up over a period, during which you are learning and building your knowledge and skills, step-by-step and reflecting on your learning as you go. If you reflect on your life in the military, those accomplishments that meant so much to you are likely to have taken perseverance and resilience and in managing to emerge successfully through those times then it seems logical to suggest you can do it again.

One of the biggest challenges can be to get the confidence balance right. So, you know your stuff and you are comfortable in displaying your skill and knowledge. But what if you're too comfortable in display, but this isn't really backed up with skill and knowledge? Maybe, all the display is just your own view of something or your interpretation. Then you're in dodgy territory because you're likely to come across as over-confident or as McGee (2020) calls it – "deluded". Have a look at the matrix below, and being very honest, where on the matrix are you at the present time? The optimum position and the one that you should aim for is to be high in competence and high in confidence.

Confidence and Competence matrix (McGee 2020: 31)

High		
	Desperately Deluded.	You are Destined for success.
	You need help.	You're not achieving your potential.
Low	Competence	**High**

(Confidence on vertical axis; Competence on horizontal axis)

So, according to the matrix if you're destined for success, well done. If you're not quite there yet well done too, as acknowledging your limitations is the first steps to success, and dipping into this book will be able to help you to develop your skills and suggest ways of making a successful transition to Civvy Street.

PROBLEM SOLVING

If problem solving is the process of finding solutions to complex or difficult situations (Oxford Dictionary 2007), then we wouldn't mind betting that you'll already be relatively competent at this skill. Your military training and service will have offered numerous opportunities for you to develop and display your problem-solving skills. Having robust problem-solving skills can be a great benefit when applying for civilian careers or for further training, so be sure to include this on your CV. Problems and challenges face many people at work every day. A fundamental part of a leadership or management role is to be able to define problems and find ways of solving them. Defining a problem is more complex than it first appears. Some problems might be obvious, but others may be buried in a set of symptoms. For example, if there are relationship issues in your team, you might believe the problem to be with one or more of the individuals, whereas, if you analyse the issue more, you might discover that the problem is a lack of direction from the leadership, or a lack of staff training. You would be able to recognise this if you consider the problem from different perspectives. There are numerous models for problem solving; you may have your own that is tried and trusted. Most problem-solving models are variations of a theme around five points:

- Defining the problem
- Analyse the problem
- Consider the options for solving the problem
- Implement the problem-solving procedure/s
- Review and amend options as necessary.

Whatever model you allude to, this is a skill that is sought after in many civilian contexts.

LEADERSHIP

Leadership is demonstrated in a variety of ways depending on the environment and context in which it is being displayed. For example, parents employ leadership traits when encouraging their children to attend sports practice. Similarly, a nursing ward sister will demonstrate leadership strategies and skills when managing the care of the patients on the ward. You will be able to reflect on your military career and on the leadership skills you've employed yourself and those that you will have witnessed others displaying. There are two concepts at the centre of each leadership task:

- A target or a goal
- Mobilising oneself and other people towards this goal.

A simple definition of leadership is: "The ability to mobilise, coordinate, motivate, direct and manage people towards achieving a specific goal". (Baisley 2016: 3) There are lots of opportunities on Civvy Street that require good leadership skills. Being able to demonstrate the transferability of your distinct leadership skills will enhance any applications you make to training providers and employers.

COACHING AND MENTORING

The terms coaching and mentoring are often used in the same context and they are sometimes used interdependently as well as distinctly. There are many different definitions of each of these terms, and they share similar characteristics. For example, they are each to do with supporting people, normally in some sort of improvement, either personally or professionally. They both require some degree of skill set on behalf of the coach or the mentor, but this is where they differ. There are subtle nuances between the coach and the mentor. A coach is someone who may or may not have had extensive experience in the speciality in which they are coaching. They may not be in a senior position to those they are coaching, but a coach will be trained in the art of coaching, in getting the best out of people, in encouraging and motivating. A good coach will be able to get the person they are coaching to critically reflect on their skills and limitations and, in that reflection, be able to become self-motivated. A mentor might also have these skills, but the subtle difference is that the mentor will probably have a good knowledge and understanding of the subject/area that the mentee is concerned with. So, a mentor may be a senior employee or a manager. Different organisations may use these terms slightly differently, but we argue that you'll have both coaching and mentoring skills that you'll have built up during your military career and they are very transferable. There are certificated courses and degree programmes that focus on coaching and mentoring; similarly, there are lots of opportunities in civilian organisations for coaches and mentors. Therefore, being able to demonstrate how your skills in these areas are transferable will be useful to any future applications you make.

TEAM WORKING

Working as part of a team and leading or managing a team are two of the skills very often mentioned on application forms and person specifications for jobs. You'll have skills in these areas from your previous work and learning experiences. Being part of a team requires certain types of communication skills, for example: having consideration for the other team members' points of view, knowing how to offer your opinion, getting involved in team events etc. Whereas, leading a team requires other skills associated with leadership. Employers often look for people who can do both and be able to demonstrate this. Building a team requires a consideration of complementary skills – there is no point in having a team where each of the members' strengths are in the same area. A successful team is made up of members who possess strengths in different areas, very similar to the military. Being able to recognise this and acknowledge your part in the team might be useful when considering this as a transferable skill.

MOTIVATION

Being self-motivated and being able to motivate others are very sought-after skills on Civvy Street. You will have experienced a significant degree of training to become motivated within the military and this will stand you in good stead on Civvy Street. However, when you were serving, your motivation was likely to have been towards a shared aim, or a goal or target that had to be met. One of our veterans told us that "in the military aggression is rewarded and it is how things get done". Well, showing aggression is not likely to get things done on Civvy Street, quite the opposite in fact. Different people demonstrate motivation in different ways, and if your experience has been that aggression is a demonstration of motivation then some of the civilians you work and learn with will probably seem a bit lacklustre when it comes to being motivated. One of our other veterans told us that the biggest challenge for them was in understanding the motivations of the tutors at the university to which they were applying. They said that they felt the tutors just didn't seem to help them or get them motivated to start their course. The university tutors are likely to argue that it's up to the individual to demonstrate self-motivation in driving their own application to the programme. This is an example of what several of the veterans responding to our research told us, that you need to be self-motivated and do things yourself. The above is adapted from John Adair's book on motivation that you might find interesting.

There are numerous other skills that you'll have in bucket loads, for example: *Communication, information technology, organisation, time management, analytical skills, numeracy and project management etc.* all of which are valuable, both to you and to any future employer in Civvy Street. There will be other, more specialised trade skills too that you may possess that you will be able to transfer. Although we have set each of these skills apart and analysed them independently, they are inter-connected, and some will mesh with others to some degree. For example, Communication features in almost all the other skills and if you were in a position of leadership, the skills you displayed carrying out leadership tasks are likely to be repeated when organising or project managing. Be sure to recognise this on any applications and conversations you have with prospective training providers and employers, as they might not understand just how skilled you are, and only you can inform them of this.

MILITARY EXPERIENCE AS PRIOR LEARNING

So, we argue that your military experience has provided you with a skill set that is extremely valuable to many employers, and we are optimistic that more employers will see the benefits to employing military veterans. The Armed Forces Covenant is testament to this, as are incentives such as the Troops to Teaching programme (**www.getintoteaching.education.gov.uk**) and the NHS Step into Health programme (**www.militarystepintohealth. nhs.uk**) to name just two. We expand on these career opportunities and signpost to key contacts later in the book. Whether you are considering going into further education (college) or higher education (university), or if you are thinking of getting a civilian job, we believe that by making the most of the skills and knowledge you have built up will strengthen your application – "hidden within all students . . . lies a mass of knowledge and skills acquired in a wide variety of ways and distributed between heart, head and hands . . . the task of the learner and the coach is to bring this mass out into the open and to use it for the benefit of the student"(Trowler. 1996. 1). Therefore, we will explore the notions of prior experiential learning and prior certificated learning and suggest how you can make the best of your experiences to support your application to college or university.

What is learning from experience?

The notion of experience is complex and has been considered by a few philosophers, whilst others have avoided the concept as it proved difficult and ambiguous. It is "almost impossible to establish a definitive view" of experience (Boud et al 1993: 6). The Collins Dictionary has several definitions of "experience":

- "experience is knowledge or skill in a particular job or activity, which you have gained because you have done that job or activity for a long time"
- "experience is used to refer to past events, knowledge, and feelings that make up someone's life or character"
- "an experience is something that you do or that happens to you, especially something important that affects you"
- "if you experience a particular situation, you are in that situation or it happens to you"
- "if you experience a feeling, you feel it or are affected by it".

Each of these definitions suggest that an experience is a meaningful situation, it is not merely an observation or an event that has occurred in which you played a passive part. An experience involved active participation and the 'learner' plays the most important part.

PRIOR EXPERIENTIAL LEARNING

Most universities offer accreditation of prior experiential learning or APEL. Some might refer to it as Recognition of Prior Learning or RPL. This is the process where you seek university credits for your learning that has taken place from a range of different experiences and is often personal, informal, and not necessarily part of a structured programme. Universities recognise that knowledge, skills and abilities that you develop through this type of learning can be equal to those gained by students on traditional formal courses in universities and colleges. If you have covered the content of a university or college unit or module (or several) by previous work and life experiences, APEL/RPL is a good way to access a programme. You will need to demonstrate what the learning experience was and how it maps to the learning outcomes of the programme to which you are applying. University and college staff will help you with this. Most universities have an APEL/RPL entry route to many courses; the following chart gives an idea of some of the UK universities that are offering APEL/RPL:

University	Details – What the university says on its website
University of Cumbria	If you feel you have covered the content of a module/ modules via your work/ life experience, APEL is a way to provide the evidence to show this and to gain credit for it. You will need to establish the learning experience (i.e. what was the experience?) and then identify the learning which has taken place (i.e. what did you learn from your experience?).
University of Durham	APEL is a way of granting credit to an individual student who can demonstrate that the learning they have acquired through life experiences (such as uncertificated training or workplace learning) is equivalent to the achievement of the learning outcomes for a specific module or Level of study. As such, APEL focuses on the learning gained through experience, rather than the experience per se.
University of Chester	The University may grant you exemption from parts of a programme by recognising qualification and experience you may have gained previously. This is called accreditation of prior credited/ certified learning (APCL) or accreditation of prior experiential learning (APEL). This can only be granted if you can provide evidence of achievement which is assessed by the University as equivalent to the module or modules that are being exempted.
University of Glasgow	The University of Glasgow invites applications to its degree programmes from all prospective students who possess the ability, knowledge and experience required to benefit from them. The University demonstrates its commitment to this aspiration through its widening participation schemes, its arrangements for credit accumulation and transfer, and the accreditation of prior learning.
Northern Ireland colleges and universities	The Department for Employment and Learning (DEL) is committed to the principle that higher education, and Foundation Degrees (FDs) in particular, are open to all those who have the ability to benefit from higher education. To help bring this about it wishes to encourage more people, who may have less in the way of formal qualifications, to consider applying for places in higher education based on accredited prior experiential learning (APEL). The Quality Assurance Agency for Higher Education (QAA) defines APEL as a process through which learning achieved outside education

University	Details – What the university says on its website
	or training systems is assessed and, as appropriate, recognised for academic purposes. The goal of APEL therefore is to value, recognise and assess an individual's experiential learning with a view to awarding credit for learning that occurs from life and work experiences.
Swansea University	For the purpose of this document, the Accreditation of Prior Learning, or Recognition of Prior Learning, signifies the process by which this University (and many others) gives recognition to learning achieved by an individual before entry to a programme of study at Swansea. At Swansea, the term covers the following: **Credit Transfer** – Where the credits or qualification have been awarded by a UK higher education institution as part of a formal qualification or by a non-UK institution as part of an equivalent qualification; **Accreditation of Prior experiential Learning (APeL)** – where learning gained through experience is assessed and recognised.

This list demonstrates that APEL/RPL requirements of each of the universities identified here is similar, that is due to them having to offer APEL/RPL according to the national academic standards. We would therefore recommend that if you are considering using your experience to access further training, you should contact your local university or college and ask what the APEL requirements are for the programme you are interested in following. If you don't live near an institute of further or higher education, you might consider the open university or other virtual/distance education providers.

TYPES OF EXPERIENCE AND LEARNING FOR ACCREDITATION

Having served in the military you are likely to have been exposed to situations and circumstances that called on you to push boundaries that you didn't know you had. We have set out below some of the experience you may have encountered and how the skills involved in the experience could be considered for APEL, but there will be many more. We have mapped the experience to a typical college/university programme criteria as an example.

Experience	Learning outcomes for university/college programme
Where you would weigh up and be able to describe the differences in political/ethnic/ essence of an organisation	Analyse the cultural diversity of an organisation.
Where you could give examples with detail of where you have led a significant change within the military and supported other colleagues through this change.	Demonstrate how you have acted as a change agent and supported staff through the change.
Where you will understand the different styles of leadership – democratic, autocratic, laissez faire etc – and weigh up the pros and cons of each and then know what your preferred style is.	Critically reflect on your leadership style and skills.
Where you would be able to describe a specific project/task that you have managed and put a value on the skills required – time management, prioritising, delegation etc	Evaluate the key skills required when managing a project.
Where you would have specific objectives from the military and would need to put these into practice.	Identify key considerations when interpreting organisational objectives for practical implementation.

We discuss in more detail later what is meant by terms such as: "critically reflect", "evaluate" etc as these require you to provide different accounts, but essentially, the events you have experienced will give you ample opportunity to convert them into credits.

ACCREDITATION OF PRIOR CERTIFICATED LEARNING (APCL)

APCL is like APEL, but the distinction is that APCL offers the opportunity for claiming credit when you have previously gained **certificates** from another institution that is comparable to the award for which you want to apply. The prior certification should be awarded by a recognised academic institution so that it assures the quality of assessment and assessed learning experience. You would apply to the college or university in the same way and state that you have certificates that you would like them to consider as part of your application. Some education institutes put a time limit on certificates, so for example, they may require that any certificates be no older than 10 years. However, if you have a Higher National Certificate that you were awarded 15 years ago, you may still be entitled to apply for APCL; it is always worth discussing this with college and university tutors responsible for applications. So, it's worth digging any certificates out that you have been awarded from military courses and asking if you are able to get APCL for any of them.

PROFESSIONAL AND STATUTORY BODIES

A professional body is an organisation that maintains an oversight of the knowledge, skills, conduct and practice of a profession or occupation; for example, The Royal College of Nursing (RCN) is the professional body for Nursing, and the Institute of Mechanical Engineers (iMechE) the professional body for engineers. A statutory body is appointed by the Government and established by an act of Parliament with the purpose of giving advice and offering consultation, considering data and making judgements in certain areas, for example, English Heritage, Environment Agency and the Health and Safety Executive, to name just a few.

The Chartered Management Institute is the chartered body for management and leadership; it offers accreditation for leadership and management courses and works with the military in accrediting programmes.

"CMI works extensively with the Army to accredit many career-progression courses. Most of the courses we accredit do not require you to undertake any additional work and in the majority of cases we can award qualifications to those who have completed courses since 2010 – If you have undertaken any of the qualifications listed below during your time in the Army since 2010, you will be eligible to apply for a CMI accredited qualification. Upon accreditation you will also receive 12 months' free CMI membership, which offers a host of benefits to support you in your career." (https://www.managers.org.uk/education-and-learning/qualifications/armed-forces/army/)

The Chartered Management Institute has also signed the Armed Forces Covenant, so it is likely that you will receive a favourable response to any approach you make to the Institute.

WHAT IS LEARNING?

Adapting to life on Civvy Street will be a challenge. It's bound to be, as you've been living an extraordinary life during your time serving in the forces. In this chapter we discuss the notion of learning and offer some explanations and suggestions of what learning is and how you can begin to develop your learning skills to support you in transition to civilian life. Below are two statements often heard when the topic of learning is being considered. Have a think about each of them and decide which one is nearest to your own view.

What you don`t know by now, you`ll never know

You learn something new every day

So, if you relate more to the first statement, you may feel that your learning is complete, that there is not anything more for you to learn. Your experience in the forces has undoubtedly provided you with learning opportunities that most people could only imagine. However, if you close yourself off to more learning opportunities, resettlement will be much more difficult. We argue that to have experienced life in the armed forces, you already have a significant toolbox of skills, so to add more civilian skills and knowledge to this existing skill set can only be to your benefit. We therefore advocate for the second statement, or at least ask that you remain open minded to new learning opportunities. When we were interviewing veterans for this book, each of those who had gone on to have successful careers following their military career talked of not being embarrassed by having to learn something new. One veteran spoke of feeling a bit like a duck out of water initially when they had enrolled on a college course. They felt that they had two types of learning to get to grips with. One was the subject of the course – in this case it was the Certificate in Education course – but the other was the more challenging type and was described by them as learning to fit in with other students. In this chapter we look at what learning is and you have the opportunity to complete the Honey and Mumford learning styles questionnaire to identify what sort of learner you are.

WHY IT MIGHT BE USEFUL TO KNOW ABOUT LEARNING

If the Covid-19 pandemic has taught us anything, it is that the world has changed and is changing. People are being made redundant as employers grapple with keeping their business afloat. Services are being streamlined and managers are having to make contingency plans on a daily (sometimes hourly) basis. Similarly, training providers are making changes to the way they deliver their programmes and courses, which is creating opportunities for new ways of learning and training. There has been a keener emphasis on distance learning, for example, where the learner is in control of their own learning to a larger extent. We thought it would be useful, therefore, to discuss the notion of learning and to look at some of the different learning methods and styles. You will be no stranger at all to learning as you'll have experienced basic military training as well as subsequent training based on your role in the military. But the type of learning that will be available on Civvy Street is different, even some of the language will be different – try asking the person at the college canteen for an egg banjo!

So, if you do decide to enrol onto a college or university course – and we talk more about the details of this later – it will probably be beneficial if you try to understand some of the key aspects of the learning process.

WHAT DO WE MEAN BY LEARNING?

There are many different views, definitions, and theories about learning. There is also a vast amount of literature and research, usually in educational psychology texts, about the nature of learning. You will have your own ideas of what learning means to you and if you choose to read more about learning, some theories and definitions will make more sense to you than others. Whichever ideas seem to make sense to you, there are some fundamental principles that underpin the general notion of learning. For example, learning is about change; this might be the change experienced because of grasping a new skill or of altering an attitude or view on something.

Learning something is usually permanent as it has normally been engaged with intentionally. If we read a news article or a book, or even listen to a radio report, we have set about with the intention to understand something better or find out something new.

Learning can also take place very successfully by experience. We learn to drive a car by driving a car and although there is a theory test, learning to drive is a very practical, experiential event. There are some practical scenarios that are best learnt from trying something out. Trial and error learning can be highly effective, but this relies on the learner knowing what the error is and when it occurred, so you might argue that you need some understanding before the real learning takes place.

Learning theorists normally separate the art of learning into three main groups, sometimes called domains. These groups are: psychomotor, cognitive and affective.

> *Psychomotor*: This learning domain focuses on the practical element of learning and the skills that are concerned with physical dexterity. For example, decorating a house or using a sewing machine. Both learning scenarios require some underpinning knowledge, but largely they are physical skills that require a practical approach.

> *Cognitive*: Cognitive learning is about thinking and knowing. How, why, what, where and when are the thinking skills that are included in the cognitive domain. For example, explaining how an engine works or being able to state how disease affects the body. Both situations require knowledge and a thought process.

> *Affective*: This domain is about feelings, emotions and attitudes. It is the learning that considers and relates to the learner's interests, perceptions and motivations, for example, listening respectfully to others, receiving phenomena – willingness to hear and remember.

ACTION LEARNING

When learning is part of a continual process of finding out something new and reflecting on this in a supportive group of colleagues with the common aim of getting something done, this is action learning. It is where people in the group learn new things, but also learn from each other. It is very much a collaborative process that recognises the nuances of the members of the group and appreciates the strengths they each bring to the group (Brockbank and McGill 2004).

WORK BASED LEARNING

Work based learning is generally interpreted as working and learning being coincident. That learning is influenced by work tasks and, in turn, work is influenced by the type of learning that occurs. Learners are workers, and workers are learners. Employees need to be able to recognise this and to manage both roles. It is the underpinning theory of the apprenticeship scheme, where a day release from work to attend study is intended to bring the knowledge and theory to the practical element of the workplace (Boud and Solomon 2003).

LIFELONG LEARNING

Education has undergone many changes over the past years, and one could argue, continues to do so. The Covid pandemic has created new challenges for the educators and education policy makers. The term lifelong learning has never been more relevant. We argue that the shift in emphasis from education and onto learning could create opportunity rather than challenge. To be able to manage what we each as individuals learn is a powerful skill as the education sector tries to grapple with the inevitable changes that occur politically and socially. Learning is like breathing, it is amongst the most basic of human traits and is integral to our survival (Jarvis et al 2004). To be able to develop an openness to learning will create opportunities that would have previously been missed. Drawing on one of the interviews we had with a veteran during the writing of this book, led us to realise that the resettlement process is helped significantly by a willingness to learn and not to feel embarrassed by having to do so. We don't suggest that you actively seek out new learning opportunities every day, although we struggle to see a significant problem with this; but rather we ask that you develop an open mindedness to learning opportunities. Lifelong learning is a skill that once mastered can be a major support mechanism for your journey into Civvy Street.

OPEN AND DISTANCE LEARNING

When describing the notions of open and distance learning, it is probably useful to describe what we mean by closed learning. The learning that takes place in an institute such as a school, college or university could be referred to as closed learning. The student attends and is faced with several classes or lectures at which they are supposed to learn something. Successful learning by this method relies on the student being able to maintain the same pace as the teacher or tutor, and that they can learn by listening or taking part in whatever classroom scenario they are faced with. Open learning is different in terms of it being student-led. The student has a much bigger role in how the learning takes place. There may be a face-to-face tutorial, but most of the learning that takes place depends on the student identifying ways and means of obtaining the information they need to in order to fulfil the criteria for their award. This might mean searching literature or researching subjects etc.

There are many more different ways and types of learning, and many books have been written on learning methods. Your military experience would have undoubtably provided you with various types of learning: maybe you attended closed learning "classroom" courses, maybe you learnt on the battlefield; whatever your experiences you will have developed a learning style that has helped in your military career. We now want you to identify what sort of learner you really are. You may have had the opportunity to only learn in a certain way, so now is your opportunity to find out how you learn best and what the underpinning characteristics are of that learning style. We argue that in identifying and exploring your optimum learning style you are providing yourself with a robust tool for your progression through training or in a Civvy Street career.

WHAT SORT OF LEARNER ARE YOU?

There are several learning styles questionnaires that offer a guide as to the type of learning that suits you best. We have provided the Honey and Mumford learning styles questionnaire for you to complete. This is an opportunity to identify how you learn best. You might already have an idea, but by completing this questionnaire honestly, you'll be able to determine your preferred learning style.

Learning Styles Questionnaire (Honey and Mumford 1986)

There is no time limit to this questionnaire. It will probably take you 15-20 minutes. The accuracy of the results depend on how **honest** you are. **There are no right or wrong answers**.

If you agree more than you disagree with a statement, put a tick by it.

If you disagree more than you agree, put a cross by it.

Be sure to mark each item with either a tick or cross.

- ❏ 1. I have strong beliefs about what is right and wrong, good and bad.
- ❏ 2. I often act without considering the possible consequences.
- ❏ 3. I tend to solve problems using a step-by-step approach.
- ❏ 4. I believe that formal procedures and policies restrict people.
- ❏ 5. I have a reputation for saying what I think, simply and directly.
- ❏ 6. I often find that actions based on feelings are as sound as those based on careful thought and analysis.
- ❏ 7. I like the sort of work where I have time for thorough preparation and implementation.
- ❏ 8. I regularly question people about their basic assumptions.
- ❏ 9. What matters most is whether something works in practice.
- ❏ 10. I actively seek out new experiences.
- ❏ 11. When I hear about a new idea or approach, I immediately start working out how to apply it in practice.
- ❏ 12. I am keen on self-discipline such as watching my diet, taking regular exercise, sticking to a fixed routine, etc.

❏ 13. I take pride in doing a thorough job.

❏ 14. I get on best with logical, analytical people and less well with spontaneous, "irrational" people.

❏ 15. I take care over the interpretation of data available to me and avoid jumping to conclusions

❏ 16. I like to reach a decision carefully after weighing up many alternatives.

❏ 17. I am attracted more to novel, unusual ideas than to practical ones.

❏ 18. I don't like disorganised things and prefer to fit things into a coherent pattern.

❏ 19. I accept and stick to laid down procedures and policies so long as I regard them as an efficient way of getting the job done.

❏ 20. I like to relate my actions to a general principle.

❏ 21. In discussions I like to get straight to the point.

❏ 22. I tend to have distant, rather formal relationships with people at work.

❏ 23. I thrive on the challenge of tackling something new and different.

❏ 24. I enjoy fun-loving, spontaneous people.

❏ 25. I pay meticulous attention to detail before reaching a conclusion.

❏ 26. I find it difficult to produce ideas on impulse.

❏ 27. I believe in coming to the point immediately.

❏ 28. I am careful not to jump to conclusions too quickly.

❏ 29. I prefer to have as many resources of information as possible – the more data to think-over the better.

❏ 30. Flippant people who do not take things seriously enough usually irritate me.

❏ 31. I listen to other people's points of view before putting my own forward.

❏ 32. I tend to be open about how I'm feeling.

❏ 33. In discussions I enjoy watching the manoeuvrings of the other participants.

❏ 34. I prefer to respond to events on a spontaneous, flexible basis rather than plan things out in advance.

❏ 35. I tend to be attracted to techniques such as network analysis, flow charts, branching programs, contingency planning, etc.

❏ 36. It worries me if I must rush out a piece of work to meet a tight deadline.

❏ 37. I tend to judge people's ideas on their practical merits.

❏ 38. Quiet, thoughtful people tend to make me feel uneasy.

❏ 39. I often get irritated by people who want to rush things.

❏ 40. It is more important to enjoy the present moment than to think about the past or future.

❏ 41. I think that decisions based on a thorough analysis of all the information are sounder than those based on intuition.

❏ 42. I tend to be a perfectionist.

❏ 43. In discussions I usually produce lots of spontaneous ideas.

❏ 44. In meetings I put forward practical, realistic ideas.

❏ 45. Often, rules are there to be broken.

❏ 46. I prefer to stand back from a situation.

❏ 47. I can often see inconsistencies and weaknesses in other people's arguments.

❏ 48. On balance I talk more than I listen.

❏ 49. I can often see better, more practical ways to get things done.

❏ 50. I think written reports should be short and to the point.

❏ 51. I believe that rational, logical thinking should win the day.

❏ 52. I tend to discuss specific things with people rather than engaging in social discussion.

❏ 53. I like people who approach things realistically rather than theoretically.

❏ 54. In discussions I get impatient with irrelevancies and digressions.

❏ 55. If I have a report to write I tend to produce lots of drafts before settling on the final version.

❏ 56. 1 am keen to try things out to see if they work in practice.

❏ 57. I am keen to reach answers via a logical approach.

❏ 58. I enjoy being the one that talks a lot.

❏ 59. In discussions I often find I am the realist, keeping people to the point and avoiding wild speculations.

❏ 60. I like to ponder many alternatives before making up my mind.

❏ 61. In discussions with people I often find I am the most dispassionate and objective.

❏ 62. In discussions I'm more likely to adopt a "low profile" than to take the lead and do most of the talking.

❏ 63. I like to be able to relate current actions to a longer term, bigger picture.

❏ 64. When things go wrong, I am happy to shrug it off and "put it down to experience".

❏ 65. I tend to reject wild, spontaneous ideas as being impractical.

❏ 66. It's best to think carefully before taking action.

❑ 67. On balance I do the listening rather than the talking.
❑ 68. I tend to be tough on people who find it difficult to adopt a logical approach.
❑ 69. Most times I believe the end justifies the means.
❑ 70. I don't mind hurting people's feelings so long as the job gets done.
❑ 71. I find the formality of having specific objectives and plans stifling.
❑ 72. I'm usually one of the people who puts life into a party.
❑ 73. I do whatever is expedient to get the job done.
❑ 74. I quickly get bored with methodical, detailed work.
❑ 75. I am keen on exploring the basic assumptions, principles and theories underpinning things and events.
❑ 76. I'm always interested to find out what people think.
❑ 77. I like meetings to be run on methodical lines, sticking to laid down agenda, etc.
❑ 78. I steer clear of subjective or ambiguous topics.
❑ 79. I enjoy the drama and excitement of a crisis.
❑ 80. People often find me insensitive to their feelings.

Scoring and Interpreting the Learning Styles Questionnaire:

The Questionnaire is scored by awarding one point for each ticked item. There are no points for crossed items. Simply indicate on the lists below which items were ticked by circling the appropriate question number.

Circle the numbers in the columns below that correspond to the ticked numbers in the questionnaire above.

2	7	1	5
4	13	3	9
6	15	8	11
10	16	12	19
17	25	14	21
23	28	18	27
24	29	20	35
32	31	22	37
34	33	26	44
38	36	30	49
40	39	42	50
43	41	47	53
45	46	51	54

Activist	Reflector	Theorist	Pragmatist
48	52	57	56
58	55	61	59
64	60	63	65
71	62	68	69
72	66	75	70
74	67	77	73
79	76	78	80

Now count up how many you've circled in each column. The more circles you have in the column indicates the degree to which you align with that style. So, for example if you've circled 6 in activist column, 13 in reflector column, 12 in theorist column and 7 in pragmatist column, you are likely to learn best as a reflector and theorist, and less likely as pragmatist or activist. Now you can read on to identify more of each of the styles.

LEARNING STYLES – GENERAL DESCRIPTIONS

Activists

Activists like to involve themselves wholeheartedly and without bias in new experiences. They live in the here and now. They are usually open-minded to new ideas and are very rarely sceptical. This approach tends to make them enthusiastic about anything new or unusual. Their philosophy is: "I'll try anything once". An activist tends to act first with little thought to any long-term issues and considers any consequences afterwards. They like to fill their life with activity. Any problems that they come across they normally tackle by brainstorming. They tend to be continually looking for excitement; as soon as the excitement from one activity has died down, they are busy looking for the next. An activist thrives on the challenges of new experiences but are easily bored with implementation and the longer-term monotony of the familiarity of the project. They tend to be gregarious, finding it easy to involve themselves with others but like the limelight to shine on them in doing so.

Activists learn best when:

- There are new experiences/problems/opportunities from which to learn
- They can engross themselves in short "here and now" activities such as business games, competitive teamwork tasks, role-playing exercises
- There is excitement/drama/crisis and things chop and change with a range of diverse activities to tackle
- They have a lot of the limelight/high visibility, i.e. they can "chair" meetings, lead discussions, and give presentations
- They can generate ideas without constraints of policy or structure or feasibility
- They are thrown in at the deep end with a task they think is difficult, i.e., when set a challenge with inadequate resources and adverse conditions
- They are involved with other people, i.e. bouncing ideas off them, solving problems as part of a team
- It is appropriate to "have a go".

Activists learn least from, and may react against, activities where:

- Learning involves a passive role, i.e. listening to lectures, monologues, explanations, statements of how things should be done, reading, watching
- They are asked to stand back and not be involved
- They are required to assimilate, analyse, and interpret lots of "messy" data
- They are required to engage in solitary work, i.e. reading, writing, thinking on their own
- They are asked to assess beforehand what they will learn, and to appraise afterwards what they have learned
- They are offered statements they see as "theoretical", i.e. explanation of cause or background

- They are asked to repeat essentially the same activity repeatedly, i.e. when practising
- They have precise instructions to follow with little room for manoeuvre
- They are asked to do a thorough job, i.e. attend to detail, tie up loose ends, dot the i's, cross t's.

Summary of Activists' strengths:

- Flexible and open minded
- Happy to have a go
- Happy to be exposed to new situations
- Optimistic about anything new and therefore unlikely to resist change.

Summary of weaknesses:

- Tendency to take the immediately obvious action without thinking
- Often take unnecessary risks
- Tendency to do too much themselves and hog the limelight
- Rush into action without sufficient preparation
- Get bored with implementation/consolidation.

Key questions for activists:

- Shall I learn something new, i.e. that I didn't know/couldn't do before?
- Will there be a wide variety of different activities? (I do not want to sit and listen for more than an hour at a stretch!)
- Will it be OK to have a go/let my hair down/make mistakes/have fun?
- Shall I encounter some tough problems and challenges?
- Will there be other like-minded people to mix with?

Reflectors

Reflectors pontificate. They like to stand back to ponder experiences and observe them from many different perspectives and viewpoints. They enjoy collecting data, both first-hand and from others and from different sources. They prefer to analyse it thoroughly before coming to any conclusion. The thorough collection and analysis of data about experiences and events is what counts to reflectors so they tend to postpone reaching definitive conclusions for as long as possible. This may come across as delaying or being unnecessarily slow, but their philosophy is to be cautious. They are thoughtful people who like to consider all possible angles and implications before making a move. They prefer to take a back seat in confrontations, meetings, and discussions. They much prefer to observe other people in action rather than join the action themselves. They listen, often intently, to others and need to get the essence of the discussion before making their own points. They tend to prefer to adopt a low profile and have a slightly distant, tolerant, unruffled air about them. When they act it is part of a wider picture which includes the past as well as the present and others' observations as well as their own.

Reflectors learn best from activities where:

- They are allowed or encouraged to watch/think/chew over activities
- They can stand back from events and listen/observe, i.e. observing a group at work, taking a back seat in a meeting, watching a film or video
- They can think before acting, to assimilate before commencing, i.e. time to prepare, a chance to read in advance a brief giving background data
- They can carry out some painstaking research, i.e. investigate, assemble information, and probe to get to the bottom of things
- They can review what has happened, what they have learned
- They are asked to produce carefully considered analyses and reports
- They are helped to exchange views with other people without danger, i.e. by prior agreement, within a structured learning experience

- They can reach a decision in their own time without pressure and tight deadlines.

Reflectors learn least from, and may react against, activities where:

- They are "forced" into the limelight, i.e. to act as leader/chairman, to role-play in front of on-lookers.
- They are involved in situations which require action without planning.
- They are pitched into doing something without warning, i.e. to produce an instant reaction, to produce an off-the-top-of-the-head idea
- They are given insufficient data on which to base a conclusion
- They are given cut and dried instructions of how things should be done
- They are worried by time pressures or rushed from one activity to another
- In the interests of expediency, they must make short cuts or do a superficial job.

Summary of strengths:

- Careful
- Thorough and methodical
- Thoughtful
- Good at listening to others and assimilating information
- Rarely jump to conclusions.

Summary of weaknesses:

- Tendency to hold back from direct participation
- Slow to make up their minds and reach a decision
- Tendency to be too cautious and not take enough risks
- Not assertive – they aren't particularly forthcoming and have no "small talk".

Key questions for reflectors:

- Shall I be given adequate time to consider, assimilate and prepare?
- Will there be opportunities/facilities to assemble relevant information?
- Will there be opportunities to listen to other people's points of view – preferably a wide cross section of people with a variety of views?
- Shall I be under pressure to be slapdash or to extemporise?

Theorists

Theorists adapt and integrate observations into complex but logically sound theories. They think problems through in a vertical, step-by-step, logical, methodical, and sometimes forensic way. They assimilate disparate facts into coherent theories. They tend to be perfectionists who won't rest easy until things are tidy and fit into a rational scheme. They like to analyse and synthesise. They are keen on basic assumptions, principles, theories models and systems thinking. Their philosophy prizes rationality and logic. "If it's logical it's good." Questions they frequently ask are: "Does it make sense?", "How does this fit with that?", "What are the basic assumptions?". They tend to be detached, analytical and dedicated to rational objectivity rather than anything subjective or ambiguous.

Their approach to problems is consistently logical. This is their "mental set" and they rigidly reject anything that does not fit with it. They prefer to maximise certainty and feel uncomfortable with subjective judgments, lateral thinking and anything flippant.

Theorists learn best from activities where:

- What is being offered is part of a system, model, concept, theory
- They have time to explore methodically the associations and inter-relationships between ideas, events and situations
- They have the chance to question and probe the basic methodology, assumptions or logic behind something, i.e. by taking part in a question and answer session, by checking a paper for inconsistencies.

- They are intellectually stretched, i.e. by analysing a complex situation, being tested in a tutorial session, by teaching high calibre people who ask searching questions
- They are in structured situations with a clear purpose
- They can listen to or read about ideas and concepts that emphasise rationality or logic and are well argued/elegant/watertight
- They can analyse and then generalise the reasons for success or failure
- They are offered interesting ideas and concepts even though they are not immediately relevant
- They are required to understand and participate in complex situations.

Theorists learn least from, and may react against, activities where:

- They are pitch-forked into doing something without a context or apparent purpose
- They have to participate in situations emphasising emotions and feelings
- They are involved in unstructured activities where ambiguity and uncertainty are high, i.e. with open-ended problems, on sensitivity training
- They are asked to act or decide without a basis in policy, principle or concept
- They are faced with a hotchpotch of alternative/contradictory techniques/methods without exploring any in depth, i.e. as on a "once over lightly" course
- They find the subject matter platitudinous, shallow or gimmicky
- They feel themselves out of tune with other participants, i.e. when with lots of Activists or people of lower intellectual calibre.

Summary of strengths:

- Logical "vertical" thinkers
- Rational and objective

- Good at asking probing questions
- Disciplined approach.

Summary of weaknesses:

- Restricted in lateral thinking
- Low tolerance for uncertainty, disorder and ambiguity
- Intolerant of anything subjective or intuitive
- Full of "shoulds, oughts and musts".

Key questions for theorists:

- Will there be lots of opportunities to question?
- Do the objectives and programme of events indicate a clear structure and purpose?
- Shall I encounter complex ideas and concepts that are likely to stretch me?
- Are the approaches to be used and concepts to be explored "respectable", i.e. sound and valid?
- Shall I be with people of similar calibre to myself?

Pragmatists

Pragmatists are keen on trying out ideas, theories, and techniques to see if they work in practice. They positively search out new ideas and take the first opportunity to experiment with applications. They are the sorts of people who return from management courses brimming with new ideas that they want to try out in practice. They like to get on with things and act quickly and confidently on ideas that attract them. They tend to be impatient with ruminating and open-ended discussions. They are essentially practical, down to earth people who like making practical decisions and solving problems. They respond to problems and opportunities "as a challenge". Their philosophy is: "There is always a better way" and "if it works it's good".

Pragmatists learn best from activities where:

- There is an obvious link between the subject matter and a problem or opportunity on the job
- They are shown techniques for doing things with obvious practical advantages, i.e. how to save time, how to make a good first impression, how to deal with awkward people
- They have the chance to try out and practise techniques with coaching/ feedback from a credible expert, i.e. someone who is successful and can do the techniques themselves
- They are exposed to a model they can emulate, i.e. a respected boss, a demonstration from someone with a proven track record, lots of examples/anecdotes, and a film showing how it's done
- They are given techniques currently applicable to their own job
- They are given immediate opportunities to implement what they have learned
- There is a high face validity in the learning activity, i.e. a good simulation, "real" problems
- They can concentrate on practical issues, i.e. drawing up action plans with an obvious end product, suggesting short cuts, giving tips

Pragmatists learn least from, and may react against, activities where:

- The learning is not related to an immediate need they recognise/they cannot see, an immediate relevance/practical benefit
- Organisers of the learning, or the event itself, seem distant from reality, i.e. "ivory towered", all theory and general principles, pure "chalk and talk"
- There is no practice or clear guidelines on how to do it
- They feel that people are going round in circles and not getting anywhere fast enough
- There are political, managerial, or personal obstacles to implementation
- There is no apparent reward from the learning activity, i.e. more sales, shorter meetings, higher bonus, promotion.

Summary of strengths:

- Keen to test things out in practice
- Practical, down to earth, realistic
- Business-like – gets straight to the point
- Technique oriented.

Summary of weaknesses:

- Tendency to reject anything without an obvious application
- Not interested in theory or basic principles
- Tendency to seize on the first expedient solution to a problem
- Impatient with waffle
- On balance, task oriented, not people oriented.

Key questions for pragmatists:

- Will there be ample opportunities to practise and experiment?
- Will there be lots of practical tips and techniques?
- Shall we be addressing real problems and will it result in action plans to tackle some of my current problems?
- Shall we be exposed to experts who know how to/can do it themselves?

One you have identified what sort of learner you are, you can adapt learning situations to suit your preferred style. It is a good idea to complete this questionnaire every six months or so as your learning style could change the more learning you do. Remember, no style is right or wrong, and you should be pleased and proud that you've found out your own preferred way of learning. (Adapted from Reece and Walker 1998)

SUMMARY

We have discussed how the skills you have developed whilst serving in the military could serve you well in any future training and employment on Civvy Street, but it is only in demonstrating how these are transferable that can support your applications. The common notion of you being self-motivated and doing things yourself is again considered in this chapter as civilian training providers and employers will not normally be able to do things for you. Knowing how you learn is vital to getting the best out of any training or learning situation, and we've given you the opportunity to discover this. We were pleased to learn from some of the veterans taking part in our research that they are planning to use their learning credits to access university courses as, post-Covid, the workplace will need people with different skills and qualifications. Universities and colleges are adapting their offer of programmes to accommodate the need of organisations as the pandemic changes the training and employment landscape. It's worth keeping your eye on the websites of any training organisations you might be interested in.

REFERENCES

Adair, J. (1996) *Effective Motivation*. Pan books

Baisley, G. (2016) *Leadership: Management skills, social skills, communication skills*.

Boud, D., Cohen, R. and Walker, D. (1993) *Using Experience for learning*. Buckingham. OU Press

Boud, D. and Solomon, N. (2003) *Work-based learning: A newer higher education?* Buckingham. OU press.

Castle, K. (2010) *Study Skills for your MTL*. Exeter. Learning Matters.

Cottrell, S. (2003) *The Study Skills Handbook*. Basingstoke. Palgrave McMillan.

Honey, P. and Mumford, A. (1986) on Honey and Mumford learning styles. www.BusinessBalls.com

Jarvis, P., Holford, J. and Griffin, C. (2004) *The Theory and Practice of learning*. London. Routledge Falmer.

McGee, P. (2020) *Self Confidence: The remarkable truth of how a small change can boost your resilience and increase your success.* Chichester. Wiley.

McGill, I. and Brockbank, A. (2004) *The Action Learning Handbook.* London. Routledge Falmer.

Parker, A. and Stone, E. (2014) Identifying the effects of unjustified confidence versus overconfidence: lessons learned from two analytic methods. Wiley Online Library.

Reece, I. and Walker, S. (1998) A practical guide to teaching, training and learning.

Yate, M. (2017) *Knock 'em Dead: The ultimate Job search guide.* Adams Media

CHAPTER 7

PREPARING FOR FURTHER AND HIGHER EDUCATION

INTRODUCTION

In this chapter we offer some guidance on how you can prepare for a further education course at college or for a degree course at university. We've heard so often from veterans who have engaged in further education following a military career that they wish they had known more of what was expected of them prior to starting the course. Karen gives an account of her experience:

My personal experience of adapting to civilian life after spending several years as a hospital officer in the prison service was fraught with difficulties and challenges. It felt like nobody on the "outside" spoke my language. That everybody seemed to trust everyone else, which was quite an eye opener for me. No one seemed to think that any situation could end badly, most people had a huge margin for error on everything they did. It took me a long time to realise that it was me with the problem, it was me who needed to try to adapt to a civilian life of some sorts. I left the prison service with a handful of Home Office certificates, largely concerning self-defence, control and restraint training or hostage negotiation techniques, not really the skills one needs for "normal" jobs on Civvy Street. By chance, whilst I was doing some agency nurse shifts, I happened to see an advert on the hospital notice board for a college course for nurses to train to be able to teach. It took me a while to galvanise the confidence to ring the number on the advert – who would want someone who has been in prison for years (albeit the one in the uniform?). But something told me it was the right thing to do, so I did. I was invited to the college for an interview and offered a place on the course. It absolutely changed my life. But there were things I wish someone had told me before I turned up to the college on that first day for the induction to the programme. College "speak" was a foreign language, the terms the staff and other students used scared the hell out of me, but somehow, I kept going and learnt very quickly that there was support available, and I used every bit of it. There are two holes in the carpet of the student support office and those holes fit my shoe prints, I was in there so much at the start. The first and probably biggest learning event for me was the notion that to look something up in a book was not cheating. I'd developed a sense that if you didn't automatically "know" something then to have to look it up in a book was somehow an indication that you were lacking something. How naïve. Of course, to "know" something you need to find out about it, and reading is one of the best methods to do it. So, I was a regular visitor to the college library and began to develop a keen interest in finding out information and researching various ideas and concepts.

The reason I'm sharing this experience is to try to demonstrate how empowering training and gaining a qualification can be, particularly if you are unsure of what you might want to do once you've been through resettlement. I would also argue that it's never too late to start a course, either at college or at university.

Since the pandemic, the workplace is changing rapidly, and employers need a workforce that is trained in different skills and in different ways.

Further and higher education establishments have had to adapt to this and to offer courses that develop the skills that are needed by employers. In this chapter, we'll look at some specific themes around further study and what to expect if you take part in a college or university course. As you read through this part of the book, please remember that you are just as entitled as anyone else to be doing a further or higher education course. You will be just as welcome at college or university (providing you have the correct entrance qualifications), as anyone else and, once you begin your training or studies, you'll have the same opportunities as anyone else.

We feel that the struggles some service leavers and veterans appear to face when trying to access further education and training or employment are unnecessary and might seem to show contempt for the service you have given. You may have worked and lived in high risk and life-threatening situations and witnessed events and incidents that most people in civilian employment can't even imagine. But this incredible and dedicated service has provided you with some unique skills that we believe are needed now in civilian contexts more than ever.

GETTING YOUR SKILLS TOGETHER

If you're thinking about enrolling on a training programme, the points we've discussed here will help to signpost you to the information you will need. We'll discuss the differences in college and university programmes later in the chapter, but if there was one thing that would have helped me when I started training again it would have been someone giving me a guidebook about returning to training. So, we've put together some ideas and suggestions that we hope will help you to get started.

The first thing to remember is that most, if not all, of the other learners on a college and university course are there because they want to make a change to themselves. They want to: learn a new skill, change their career, get a qualification or even use their military resettlement time to develop themselves – there may well be other service leavers and military veterans on the same course as you.

You won't be the only person who feels out of your depth. That fact that you are doing a training course, or on a learning journey means that you are there to develop a skill or seek out new knowledge, so you're bound to feel less confident. The tutors will know this, they've seen learners at the start of their course who shake with nerves and feel overwhelmed by the prospect of returning to study. Similarly, they've seen learners at the start of their course who already think they know enough to pass the programme on day one and portray a sense of overconfidence. Never be afraid to say if you need help. Neither should you be afraid to make mistakes; the tutors will not expect you to be perfect at everything straight away. Many colleges run "Return to study" courses or workshops, that help with getting accustomed to training, and most universities have student learning advisors, so if you think this would be of benefit, then look them up at your nearest institution.

We make no apologies for reminding you that you have a unique and fascinating skill set that will be a great benefit to many employers, but you may need to "top" these skills up or gain a qualification in order to work in a certain area, or in a trade area, but you are starting from a very strong and knowledgeable standpoint. You may need to hone these skills in a certain way, no different to channelling your knowledge in a different area. But if your military career has taught you anything, it will be that you can approach and tackle most situations.

You might have left the military with specialist trade skills, for example: electrical, catering, medical, engineering etc. These are all incredibly useful skills for any future training or development courses you choose to take and depending on the level to which you wish to develop, these will vary depending on whether you explore the potential of going to college or university. However, in whichever training establishment you find yourself, there are a few skills and techniques that you won't necessarily have needed and may need to develop; amongst these are study skills or academic skills. So, we'll discuss some of the main themes around these areas now.

ACADEMIC AND STUDY SKILLS

When we were interviewing veterans for the case studies for this book, one conversation we had was particularly relevant to this chapter. After serving 20 years in the QAs this veteran spoke of not feeling adequately confident or competent to engage in further study. She went on to say that she wouldn't "fit in to any college or university courses" as she lacked any academic skills. Another service leaver spoke of not being "clever enough" to enrol on any further civilian training. If we consider the notions of not feeling clever enough, we'd have to ask – clever enough for what? The whole point of taking part in further training or education is that you learn as you are doing the course. No tutor expects you to have the correct number of skills or knowledge at the start of the programme, as their job is to support you to develop them as you progress. It's a real shame if veterans allow themselves to feel unworthy of taking part in civilian courses as they are missing out on some excellent opportunities. One of the other responses was that the veteran felt they didn't have any academic skills and where these too will be developed as the course progresses, it might be useful to discuss the type of academic skills you will need when embarking on a further education course. We have set out some of the main skills you'll need to start on a learning programme, but you'll develop most of your skills whilst you are engaged in study. We hope that by discussing some of these skills here, you will be able to reflect on just how much you already know. Very often it's the language that is used in colleges and universities that is off-putting. Remember, **you have as much right to be taking part in further and higher education courses as everyone else**. So, let's look at some of the "academic/study skills" that you'll need to develop.

UNDERSTANDING THE LEARNING OUTCOMES

This is quite straightforward. Every programme and each of the units or modules you'll take will have a set of learning outcomes. You'll need to complete these successfully to pass the unit. You will know what these are

at the start of your course and any taught elements of the course will help
you to complete these. The learning outcomes set out the main learning
objectives and provide you with a structure for completing the assignment.
Each of the learning outcomes should include a verb phrase and an impact
phrase. The table gives some examples of verbs used in learning outcomes;
these verbs are your first clue to what you need to do.

Verb	Definition
Define	Explain the precise meaning of a concept or idea.
Discuss	Explain an item or concept and then give details about it with supportive information. Give examples and points for and against, and explanations for the facts put forward.
Justify	Requires an answer which gives only the reasons for a position or argument. Note that the proposition to be argued may be negative, i.e. justify poor behaviour.
Analyse	Take apart an idea, concept or statement in order to consider all the factors. Answers should be methodical and logically organised.
Compare	Requires an answer which sets items side by side and shows similarities and differences. A balanced and fair objective answer is expected.
Contrast	Requires an answer which points out only the differences between the two items.
Critique or Criticise	Requires an answer which points out the benefits and favourable aspects of an item together with the weaknesses and limitations. It requires a balanced and objective answer.
Evaluate	Very similar to Discuss, but the difference is that the conclusion should make a judgement, either pro or contra the concept being discussed.
Illustrate	Requires an answer which consists mainly of examples to demonstrate or prove the subject of the question. It is often added to another instruction.
Summarise	Contains a summary of all the available information about the subject. Only the main points and not the detail. Questions of this type usually require short answers.

Have a look at the following learning outcomes taken from real programmes.

On successful completion of this course, you will be able to:

* *Evaluate how current policy can impact on the infection control protocols.*

* *Analyse the main health and safety issues for consideration by managers.*

* *Discuss some of the key theories that are relevant to the new management structure.*

On reading these initially, what are your first thoughts?

You are not expected to know the answers at the start of the course. But you will need to be able to understand what each is asking you to do, so let's break them down.

The first learning outcome asks you to "**Evaluate** how current policy can impact on the infection control protocols". This means that you should give a detailed explanation of national policy on infection control and how this then impacts on the protocol within your area. You should give examples and use supporting information, so references to the Health and Safety at work Act etc. Give examples for and against and an explanation of the argument you put forward. But the key thing here is, you need to make a judgement, or put a value on one side of the argument. The second learning outcome asks you to "**Analyse** the main health and safety issues for consideration by managers". This means that you pull apart the health and safety issues and consider all the related factors; your response to this should be methodical and logically organised. The third learning outcome asks you to "**Discuss** some of the key theories that are relevant to the new management structure", so here you would explain what some of the main theories are and then give details about them with some supportive information. Give examples and points for and against, and explanations for the facts put forward.

So, to summarise – the learning outcomes are set to offer a structure for the learner to be able to complete the unit or module. They are also a means to enable the unit to be assessed. Which brings us on to the next point.

UNDERSTANDING ASSESSMENT

Assessment is essentially your opportunity to provide the information you know about a specific subject or theme in a way that is stipulated by the awarding body or training provider. It is your opportunity to prove that you know enough about the subject to warrant passing any evaluation. Whoever marks your assessment will form a judgement based on the information you have provided. Assessments are carried out at various points of the course. Some training providers carry out an initial assessment on the learners' level of knowledge of the subject at the start of the programme. This is so that they can form a baseline of your understanding to enable them to be able to measure your progress through the course. There are two other forms of assessment commonly used by training providers: formative assessment and summative assessment.

FORMATIVE ASSESSMENT

Formative assessments are made during the course and are useful tools to inform you of how your learning is progressing and of any gaps that you need to address. They are also a means of identifying to the tutors how their teaching is influencing your learning and if they need to adapt their content or approach. The methods of formative assessment are likely to include: Questions and answers, projects, assignments, essays, and practical tests. They are not usually graded, as in a final or summative assessment as they are intended to support your learning, not grade it. The formative assessment is a real opportunity for you as a learning to gauge how your learning is doing, and to know where any gaps are. Use this to your advantage and really get to terms with any formative feedback from your tutor. Ask to have a conversation with them about their comments and really squeeze as much information as you can as this will assist you greatly in completing the rest of the assignment leading up to the summative assessment. Formative assessment/s occur at some point before the end of the course; they may be competed half-way through the programme, for example, to allow you the opportunity to improve on your weak areas prior to the final or summative assessment.

SUMMATIVE ASSESSMENT

This takes place at the end of the course or topic and is usually used for certification and award purposes. Its purpose is to identify if the learner has successfully met all the learning outcomes of the course and has reached the point of learning what was expected. It could also act as an indication of whether the learner is capable of further study at a higher level. Types of summative assessments include: End examinations, projects, assignments, tests, and essays.

When your tutor marks your assessment, they will use a grading matrix that is set against the specific level of study, so as an example, Level 3 is the equivalent of A levels and Level 7 is a Masters' Degree. They will mark your assessment and provide feedback to you on the strengths and weaknesses of the work. It is important that you consider this feedback as it will help you to improve on any further courses and assessments that you take. The feedback should be constructive, balanced, and critical, so it should identify the positive aspects of the work and give examples of where in the work this is evident. It should also identify the weaker elements of the work and make suggestions of how you can improve. You won't learn anything or progress in any way if the feedback just focuses on the good bits. Equally your confidence won't be helped if the feedback just focuses on the gaps in your knowledge, so a balanced view and judgement is what is really required by markers.

READING

This might sound obvious, but you can help yourself enormously by having a plan and a method for how you carry out reading for your course. We have already mentioned how important it is to be dipping in and out of books and journals as it is one of the most effective ways that you can develop your understanding of something. One of the biggest misunderstandings that many adult learners make is that they think they should be reading a lot of books from cover to cover. This is incorrect. You cannot possibly be expected to find the time to search the college or university library or scan the virtual library for all the stuff there is on a certain subject. The trick is to be selective in what you read. Read only the pages that appertain to your query. It helps greatly if you are clear in what your queries or quests for knowledge are, that way you'll be able to focus on exactly what you need from the start. Being able to scan read or read something to just take the key elements and focus from it is also a skill that would be useful to develop. Read from a wide range of resources, so use books, journals, current affairs accounts, research, and policy documents. Be careful when reading anything from the internet that the information is from a credible source. If you are writing about a political issue, then the latest white or green paper may be a useful source for information; a good starting point for this would be **www.gov.uk**.

REFERENCING

Whenever you take an excerpt or quote from a book or when you use someone else's ideas you need to reference this in your text. So, for example, Reece and Walker (2007) argue that students often do more reading than is necessary and should be supported to be selective. Here then, I used the idea that Reece and Walker had, in their book that was published in 2007, that students need support to be choosy with what books they read. Now if you look in the reference section you'll see that the Reece and Walker book that I used features in the list. If you were going to include a direct quote rather than summarise an idea, you'd write the quote like this: "Some courses give long reading lists and expect you to select from a range. Others give you a short list and expect you to read everything on it. If in doubt, ask your lecturer" (Cottrell 2003: 120). So, here Stella Cottrell was quoted, word for word on page 120 of her book that was published by Palgrave McMillan in 2003. Page numbers are required on all direct quotes and excerpts from books and journals. There is a lot of information on referencing and there are different referencing strategies; in the book we use the Harvard Referencing style, but your training provider will identify which referencing strategy you should use and provide you with any information you need to be able to use it correctly.

Whenever you take an idea or a quote, write the source down as you'll need the author's name, initial, date, title of the journal article or book, title of the journal, volume and issue number of the journal and page number for a direct quote. For a book you'll also need the publisher and where it was published. Look at the reference lists in this book to give you some idea. The college or university where you choose to study will have a guide to referencing; make sure you understand this as there are several ways of referencing and you'll need to use the method that your training provider prefers. As an example, Harvard Referencing is used at many UK institutions.

RESEARCH

When returning to study at college or university, it won't be long before you hear this term being used in conversations and on assignment briefs. But what does it mean? The Oxford English Dictionary claims that it is "the study of materials and sources to discover facts" (Soanes 2007: 470). If we take the concept a bit deeper, many educational texts talk of research being a search for the truth and understanding the nature of phenomena. To try to assist you in understanding what research is, we suggest that you think of research as a way of developing your knowledge around a subject, of digging deeper into some of the less obvious notions of what it is you are learning about. It also acts as a structure to allow you to read, question, discuss and do all those things that increase your understanding of a topic.

Most of the courses you undertake will require an element of research; they'll have to as the intention is, by doing them you'll learn something new. Before launching into your research, be sure to understand exactly what is required of you. What are the questions asking you to do? In her role as a university tutor, Karen has marked hundreds of student assignments and assessments, and experience has shown that one of the biggest mistakes that learners make is not reading the assignment brief correctly. We'll look at some of these in depth in the sections on further and higher education, but if there is one tip that will give you the best start on a unit or module, it is to make sure you know what the unit brief is asking you to do. You can then prepare for your learning. Once you know what you need to find out, or the questions you need to answer, you can begin to map out how you'll go about doing it. Some of the sources you'll obtain information from, and that will be in the college or university library or on-line, are:

- Books
- Academic Journals
- Government papers
- Newspapers
- Company Data
- Financial Data.

There are advantages and disadvantages to each of these methods, so using a range is usually advised. For example, a book is out of date far sooner than a journal. When you read a book, it is at least three months old, whereas a journal might be a few weeks. So, if you need to find out some up-to-date information, you're better to look at company information, government information or an article in a recent journal. However, information in a book is useful when you want to know more about the theories associated with something or to go into depth on a specific subject.

When you are researching, you are searching for new information that may or may not align with your own understanding or beliefs. Research is about doing a 360-degree scoop on the information around the subject. You'll really grapple with the topic, find out information on all the ramifications of what is going on, the positives, negatives and all the grey bits in between. You'll weigh up potential and reflect on alternatives. You'll seek out as much as possible on what has been written about these areas. You'll also look at other research that has been done on the same or similar area to that which you are studying. That's why it's good to have a plan. Set time for the reading and once you've reached that date, STOP reading and start to write your report or assignment. There is a very great tendency to keep on reading, that's normal, as your inquisitiveness will continue once you've begun, but you need to concentrate on planning and starting the writing in good time so that you don't miss the deadline. Talking of deadlines, the next section goes into more detail of this and gives you some tips for writing your assignment.

WRITING YOUR ASSIGNMENT

You're now at the stage of being able to write your assignment. We'll call it an assignment for now, but the actual piece of work that you have produced may be any of the following:

- Report
- Literature review
- Essay
- Critical reflection.

Your course information and tutors will guide you on this, and we go into it in some detail in the next sections, but essentially you'll have to complete a unit task that asks you to produce an assignment in a certain way; this is sometimes referred to as the assignment/module/ unit brief.

We think it might be useful to talk you through a typical unit so that you think about how you'd go about writing your assignment if you were completing this unit of study. Depending on which institution you are studying with, the units or modules will look different, but they will contain the same or similar information. We've written the following unit based on our knowledge and understanding of college and university courses over the last 20 years.

Unit Title: Strategic and operational considerations in your present or most recent workplace

Assignment Brief:

In completing this unit, you will have the opportunity to express ideas effectively and apply critical and analytical skills to a real work situation within the context of strategic and operational concern.

Examples of this could be:

Risk management, Governance, business management or development, public relations etc.

You will recognise the impact of positive professional working relationships and recognise and respect different perspectives.

Learning Outcomes: At the end of this unit, you will be able to:

- Critically analyse the process involved in managing risk in a given situation.
- Evaluate how organisational strategies and plans are developed in respect of workforce development and quality assurance.
- Summarise how recent policy impacts on the situation.

Assessment strategy:

A written essay (60%) for learning outcomes 1 and 2 [equivalent of 3000 words]

Summary report (40%) for learning outcome 3 [equivalent of 2000 words]

Deadline 12.00 hours May 1st 2021

Recommended reading:

Castle, K. (2010) *Study skills for your MTL*. Exeter. Learning Matters
Cottrell, S. (2003) *The study skills handbook*. Hampshire. Palgrave McMillan.
McGee, P. (2020) *Self- confidence: The remarkable truth of how a small change can boost your resilience and increase your success*. Chichester. Wiley.
Reece, I. and Walker, S. (2007) *Teaching, Training and Learning: a practical guide*. 6th Edition. Business education publishers Ltd.

A good starting point would be to look at the learning outcomes to plan your assignment. Learning outcome 1 asks you to consider a certain situation. You therefore need to think of an event or incident at work that would allow you to answer the learning outcomes. Let's use as an example a situation where you had to lead the process of moving the workforce from an office environment to working from home. This is a situation experienced during the Covid pandemic and created both challenges and opportunities for managers and employees alike. Put yourself in the position of having to lead this process for the purpose of considering this unit. If we therefore look at the learning outcomes again but this time with some suggestions in italics:

- Critically analyse the process involved in managing risk in a given situation.
  Critically analyse the process of leadership – so you'll weigh up the pros and cons of leading the change. You might look at managing change and read some literature on this. As a leader you might want to know what some theories of leading and managing change suggest. Then it asks you to consider managing risk (in managing staff to work from home). Therefore you'll consider what risks might it be necessary to consider in this situation. If staff need to work from home, these risks might include working safely at a home computer and maintaining confidentiality and privacy of information. You'll then give a critical account (weighing up the pros and cons again) of managing these risks. As a leader you might be responsible for writing and maintaining the risk assessments.

- Evaluate how organisational strategies and plans are developed in respect of workforce development and quality assurance.
  Here you will consider and put a value on the degree to which relevant organisational strategies and plans support staff development and quality assurance when staff work from home. This might involve the health and safety policy for working at computers. It might also require you to look at the staff development plan and if the working from home policy had been brought in quickly, it might mean you needed to

arrange staff development in data protection. It also asks you to consider quality assurance, so you'll provide an evaluation of how you led the monitoring of quality through the process.

- Summarise how recent policy impacts on the situation.
  If the working from home policy was brought in because of the pandemic, then you'd consider the Government advice and guidance on staff working from home and how your organisation interpreted this for practical use. It asks for a summary, not a full- blown report, so just select the main points and discuss these. We suggest that GDPR legislation and Health and Safety at work legislation would be two policies that you'd consider.

By breaking the learning outcomes down and using your chosen situation to frame your assignment, you can focus on some key areas. This then provides you with a set of topics that you can then research and shape into a written essay of 3,000 words.

PLANNING YOUR ESSAY

There are various ways of designing an essay. But the essence of what needs to be included in most essays and where it needs to feature are similar. We have suggested one structure, but there are many.

Introduction	Introduce the essay, specifically the situation in your workplace that will form the focus of the essay.
Section 1/chapter 1 – Key discussion 1	Managing risk in supporting staff to work from home
Section 2/chapter 2 – Key discussion 2	Evaluation of the Health and Safety at work policy and the data management policy

Section 3/chapter 3 – Key discussion 3	Leadership and management strategies and underpinning theory.
Conclusion	Bring together the key points that you've discussed and say how they answer the learning outcomes.

The trick to enabling the essay to flow is to provide linking sentences between the different sections or chapters. This is a skill that you'll develop as you make progress, and it is something that your tutor will help you with.

The second part of this assignment is a summary report. You could plan the written report in a similar way in terms of an introduction followed by sections that contain specific points, followed by a conclusion, but as this is a summary, then you don't need the discussion and narrative that you had in the first part of the assignment.

Your deadline for completing and submission is May 1st, so we suggest that you consider your deadline as April 21st – 10 days prior to the deadline, to allow for a thorough edit and to give you time to action any final feedback from tutors. Once you've submitted your assignment and received the feedback, make sure you understand what the marker has written, and it will help you when you complete your future assignments.

FURTHER EDUCATION

If you are thinking of doing a professional qualification or work-based certificate or diploma, you might be considering attending a further education college, or your workplace may have a partnership with a particular college for the purpose of staff development. Once you are enrolled on the college programme, you are entitled to all the benefits and services that the other students have. As we mentioned earlier, you are entitled to use the student support services; the staff in this department are fully trained and experienced in offering extra support to all students. They are also qualified to support students who have dyslexia and other learning issues. We cannot stress enough how important it is to use this service.

Some college courses allow you to use your existing certificates and qualifications, together with any prior experience, to enter a programme on a recognition of prior learning route. We discussed this in more detail earlier in the book, but it is always worth asking the course team if there is the opportunity for entry via this route. As a general principle, further education colleges tend to focus on levels 2 – 6. Level 3 is the academic level that is the equivalent of A levels and Level 6 is a Bachelor's Degree level. Some colleges also offer postgraduate (level 7) study but this level of study is normally the domain of the university.

HIGHER EDUCATION

You may be considering doing a degree or topping up your existing degree, or your employer might have staff development programmes that are accredited by a university. The main difference between further education and higher education is the level of courses provided at each. Universities normally focus on levels 6 – 8 study. Level 6 is an undergraduate degree or Bachelor's degree, level 7 is a Master's Degree and level 8 a PhD or Doctorate. Levels 7 and 8 usually require a significant amount of research, which often spans several years. Several occupations are degree occupations, where a degree is considered necessary to be able to carry out the roles effectively. Teaching and nursing are two examples of degree level professions and to provide effective qualified courses, universities and employers have forged partnerships to offer work placements for trainees on these programmes. There are an increasing number of university courses being delivered by a blended learning method. This means that the students only attend the university for part of the study time. There is more emphasis put on independent study and the student managing their own learning. The Open University (OU) is an example of distance or blended learning – on an OU course, the student has virtual support from a tutor and leads their learning themselves, attending the occasional face-to-face seminar or summer school.

Universities normally offer recognition of prior learning as entry onto several postgraduate degree programmes. We encourage you to explore this option as it could be an extremely useful way of you getting onto a degree course. The best way to find out about this is to contact the university where you are considering studying and ask about recognition of prior experiential learning (RPEL) as a route to the degree you are interested in studying. We mentioned this earlier in the book and gave some examples of the universities that offer RPEL. We want to emphasise that you are just as entitled to be on a university course as anyone else.

Having recently had a conversation with a military leaver who was applying for a university course during her final three months of service, it became evident that she was considering cancelling her application as she had not heard from the admissions department regarding her application. If we consider what we said at the start and maintain throughout this book, it is up to you to actively chase up any information or responses you require. In the military you are used to communications being clear, accurate and timely, but Civvy Street is not always like this, so, once she had telephoned the admissions department and asked them to contact her with the progress of her application, she was able to learn that her personal statement had not been passed to the programme team and so she would not be likely to have been called up at the appropriate time. The moral of this story is: colleges and universities are big organisations with separate and distinct departments that don't always "talk" to one another, so it's always best to get the name of the programme leader and the contact details and chase them up. By doing this, you place yourself firmly on the radar of the staff that are dealing with the programme – that can't be a bad thing.

SUMMARY

When we spoke to the veterans responding to the research, we learnt that they had quite different experiences in terms of education and training advice through their resettlement. Fortunately, this hadn't put some of them off applying to university courses. Most colleges and universities are quite happy to discuss on the telephone your choices and what programmes would be appropriate for you in your area of interest. Also, most education establishments have detailed websites that offer a good insight into their programme offer. The Open University and other virtual learning establishments might be the preferable choice for you, but these do rely on you being self-motivated in terms of your study time. We have been able to give you a bit of an insider's view of applying for further and higher education courses in this chapter, particularly in terms of the sorts of assessments you'll be expected to carry out and in some of the programme and learning information.

REFERENCES

Cottrell, S. (2003) *The study skills handbook*. Hampshire. Palgrave McMillan.

McGee, P. (2020) *Self- confidence: The remarkable truth of how a small change can boost your resilience and increase your success*. Chichester. Wiley.

Reece, I. and Walker, S. (2007) *Teaching, Training and Learning: a practical guide*. 6th Edition. Business education publishers Ltd.

Soanes, C. (2007) Oxford English Mini Dictionary. Oxford. OU press.

CHAPTER 8

THE CIVILIAN WORKPLACE

INTRODUCTION

In this chapter we look at some of the behaviours and traditions evident in the civilian workplace that help shape the culture of the work environment. Cultures exist wherever people come together to form a collective where there is a sense of shared purpose. Rules and regulations that are written in statute or in policy can drive or influence culture, but it is often the unwritten rules and behaviours that allow cultures to manifest and develop. There is sometimes a difference between what workplaces promote, i.e. "We always value new ideas, we treat all our staff with courtesy and respect, people are our best asset" etc. to what is deemed to be true by some staff. Of course, this has a lot to do with interpretation and some staff will interpret the workplace as supportive, respectful, fair etc. whilst others may not. Your time spent in the military will have given you a certain view of a work environment based on your experiences. You will have formed an opinion of what good leadership and management is, of what effective teamwork is, and of how workplaces function. But Civvy Street is different. The belief systems, values and taboos of the civilian workplace will probably be quite different to those that you have experienced previously. Finding a workplace that embraces a culture that you feel is right, or you feel that you can work in, will be a great advantage to you.

It will be worth putting significant time in to researching the companies or organisations you are thinking of joining to identify the type of culture that is present. For example, some workplaces have a relaxed attitude to how staff dress. If you were to visit the offices of Google or the "Innocent" drinks manufacturer or UK Fast, for instance, you will witness staff in jeans and being encouraged to sit on bean bags and visit relaxation suites etc. In contrast, if you went to IBM or to an accountancy firm you're more likely to see people in suits and working to a more formal workplace environment. You are more likely to embrace a new workplace and fit in with the work environment if you can accept and work within that culture. Working in the public sector (organisations created by Government including, for example, local authorities) is quite different to working in the private sector (owned and financed by individuals). There is very often a culture difference when, for example, an organisation is focused on making profit (for example a retailer) rather than when an organisation is not for profit (NHS) or a social enterprise. The strategic objectives of these types of organisations are quite different and this is reflected in the way they are managed and led. You will benefit greatly in getting as much information as possible about the organisation or firm you are intending to apply to prior to applying for and accepting a post within the firm. Find out what the organisation's values are. You can very often get this from the "about us" section on the organisation's information page. You can also talk to a company representative prior to applying for posts. We talk more about this in the following chapter, but most job adverts have a named person with whom you can have an informal discussion prior to completing an application. Take this opportunity and ask questions that get you the answers you need in terms of the culture of the organisation.

CHARACTERISTICS OF CIVILIAN EMPLOYMENT

There is a vast amount of literature on how organisations function etc. You might find some of it informative and useful. Laurie Mullins writes on

Management and Organisational Behaviour, Charles Handy on organisations and leadership, and David Ritzer's book on The McDonaldisation of Society offers some interesting thoughts on how organisations have adopted a McDonald's style of operating. But you might also be interested in the books by Michael Argyle. Argyle was a well-known English Social Psychologist. He was born in Nottingham in 1925 and died in 2002. He completed a Royal Airforce science course at Cambridge and trained as a navigator. After the war he studied at Emmanuel College Cambridge and went on to be one of the first early pioneers of social psychology in the UK. His book "The social psychology of work" is well worth a read. But if reading really isn't your thing, don't worry, we do discuss some of the key issues in terms of how organisations function and why they do it in a certain way in this book and in our subsequent guidebooks for Civvy Street. It was whilst talking to one of the veterans for the case studies, that we were alerted to the need for an employer's guide to recruiting and appointing military veterans, so, that will be another subsequent book in the Civvy Street series.

Organisations take a variety of forms depending on the nature of what the organisation is concerned with. Since the industrial revolution, the workplace has tended to increase in size to maximise profits and exploit other economies of scale. However, it could be argued that the digital revolution has resulted in organisations contracting as technology and machinery replace the human resource. The Covid pandemic also has had an impact on the size of organisations. One only needs to recall how the airline industry has been affected by a reduction in travellers due to the lockdown restrictions. The world of work is constantly changing, and this has an impact on individual organisations that then also must change. But because they are transforming, then this impacts on the world of work and so the cycle begins again. It is fair to say then that the workplace is in a constant state of flux (Handy, 1993). In the new (post-Covid) world the saying "survival of the fittest" could well be superseded by "survival of those most adaptable to change". And you've got all the skills to do just that as you've been adapting and changing during your service within the military, so by drawing on the notion of transferable skills that we mentioned earlier, you are well placed to use your adaptability when you engage in the civilian workplace.

THE NATURE OF ORGANISATIONS

Most if not all organisations have a function to perform as they operate to fulfil objectives that are normally not achievable by individuals. Organisations are socially constructed by specific groups using co-ordinated activities to achieve a specific purpose. There is a great diversification in organisations as they need to meet a variety of needs.

If we consider the following organisations: Local authorities, banks, leisure centres, libraries, schools, hospitals, airports, motor car manufacturers and prisons. They will each possess some common factors, for example: People, structure, and objectives. But these will change depending on the organisation as they will have different structure, management, and functions. People work together within the organisation to achieve the objectives and they do this by adhering to some sort of (leadership and management) structure, that co-ordinates the actions of the people.

As well as internal influences on an organisation, people, structures, policies etc. there are many external and environmental influences that impact on the organisation. The effectiveness of the performance of the business will depend on how these are managed.

The following demonstrates some of the external factors that provide significant challenge and opportunities for organisations:

In the UK, at least, the focus of the organisation is to deliver effectively (for example, a profit or a service), it is not the job of the organisation to be an alternative social space or a place where you go to be provided for or to promise you a job for life (Handy 1993). It could be argued that since the shift from the old "personnel" model to the "human resource" model of work, people in the workplace are considered a resource (much the same as a stapler or a delivery van) for the organisation to use as it feels fit to optimise the profit or service. Some workplaces feel quite impersonal and very task orientated. Handy (1993: 70) has argued that employment organisations have been especially useful to the Government as "delivery instruments of Government policy but now that they employ an ever-decreasing percentage of society's adults, they are less useful". This raises the question of who is supposed to look after the workers if the organisations focus more on results and targets. Trade Unions and Professional Statutory and Regulatory bodies are two types of organisation or association that claim to do this, and we discuss these briefly here.

TRADE UNIONS

You might not have had much to do with a trade union whilst serving in the military. But on Civvy Street, there are several unions that, according to the UK Gov website (**www.gov.uk**) are organisations with members who are usually workers or employees, and which exist to support these employees in the workplace. There is usually a fee for membership of a union, and this differs depending on the union. Trade union members have come together to form a union with the intention of looking after the interests of the members in several ways, for example:

- Negotiating with employers on pay and conditions of work
- Discussing large changes in the employment area, for example redundancies
- Discussing members' concerns with the employer or the employers' representatives
- Accompanying members to disciplinary hearings and grievance meetings

- Bringing to the attention of management, matters of health and safety or other threats to the members
- Providing current information regarding the trade or profession.

When you first start a new job where there is an active trade union, you are likely to be informed of who the union representatives are and who the shop steward is by the union themselves, but if not, then this is something that you'll be able to find out yourself from other staff. If you want to join a trade union, you will be asked to complete a form, and arrange payment of union fees in return for some sort of confirmation that you are a member (usually a certification of membership or a membership card). If you would like to join a union, but there doesn't appear to be an active or functioning union at your workplace, go to **www.tuc.org.uk** and you will be able to search for a union that operates within your area of work. You can be a member of a "virtual" union if there is no physical presence of a union within your specific workplace. There are advantages and disadvantages of being a member of a trade union and we list some of these here:

Advantages	Disadvantages
Support at grievance and disciplinary events.	If the union calls for strike action, you will be expected by the union to join in, even though you might not agree with striking.
Legal advice/support.	Sometimes creates an "us and them" atmosphere in the workplace between members and non-members.
Professional trade information and in some cases, professional development courses and opportunities	Unions sometimes may pit workers against the company they work for.

Ultimately, you can choose whether to belong to a trade union. You can always discontinue membership if you do initially sign up but then decide it is not for you.

PROFESSIONAL STATUTORY AND REGULATORY BODIES (PSRBS)

These are external bodies to the organisation. They formally accredit and recognise academic programmes associated with the workplace. They are also responsible for setting standards and entry criteria for professions. A regulatory body acts in the Public Interest in that they regulate certain professional activities or individual professionals. Professional bodies may also act as trade unions as well, so, for example, the British Medical Association is a professional association for medical professionals, and it is also a trade union. Some of these bodies require a payment for membership.

In contrast to the view that organisations are not places that provide any social opportunity and are merely task focused, Mullins (2002) has suggested that employees are organisational stakeholders, in the same way as consumers, finance providers and the community, and it is therefore incumbent on the employer to recognise the worker as a human being. It is certainly our experience that the degree to which the employer considers the staff depends on the workplace and on different departments within the workplace. This takes us back to one of our previous discussions that you should thoroughly research any prospective workplace or organisation prior to committing yourself to it.

LEADERSHIP AND MANAGEMENT

Having a set of values and a strategic plan is key for an organisation in order that it identifies how it supports employees in understanding the direction of the business and how it aims to reach the strategic objectives. Objectives and policies are made formal within the strategic plan of a business which will describe the purpose of the organisation and its sense of purpose and what actions it takes to implement this. However, any organisation can state what it regards as key values and how it supports and nurtures staff; whether and how it manages to put this into practice depends largely on the effectiveness of the management and leadership within the organisation. "An essential part of management is co-ordinating the activities of people and guiding their efforts towards the goals and objectives of the organisation. This involves the process of leadership and the choice of an appropriate form of behaviour. Leadership is a central feature of organisational performance" (Mullins 2002: 252).

Given our joint experiences of the military and civilian workplace as basic grade employees and having served in leadership and management positions, we are able to say with reasonable confidence that you can know everything there is to know about a subject or business and still be a poor manager. There have been arguments between academics for some time on whether good managers are born or made. We won't go into these here, but we delve a bit deeper into this fascinating argument in our book "Living and working on Civvy Street". There are many articles and books written on leadership and management, and there is much that is contested between experts and theorists. As this is a practical handbook and a guide, we intentionally don't dwell on this issue, but rather give some broad suggestions and views on leadership and management.

Much is written on the theory of Management, and if this is something you are interested to read more on, you could do worse that looking at the theories of: Fayol, Mintzberg, Hertzberg, McGreggor and F.W. Taylor. Each of these theorists agree that management is something to do with motivation and what motivates people to work, but each has a different take on the principles of management and how they are applied. Another couple of useful resources for reading about management and leadership are the websites of the Chartered Management Institute **www.managers. org.uk** and the Institute of Leadership and Management **www.i-l-m.com**

Managers are responsible and accountable for ensuring the strategic objectives of the organisation are met and they do this by: planning, organising, controlling, and motivating the workers within the organisation. But there is a massive difference in the way individual managers do this across the civilian workplace. Some managers have been in managerial positions for years and have developed their managerial skills through practical application, and others are promoted to managerial positions after passing certain qualifications. This doesn't mean that the managers who have held the position for years are not highly qualified; on the contrary, many will be. The point we are making here is that there are many different types of manager, and some will appear more supportive of staff than others; this is largely dependent on the organisation and the individual themselves. The degree to which managers carry out leadership tasks and roles is also down to the organisation – for example, in large companies, the managers are likely to have deputies and assistants and other senior staff who are responsible for some of the managerial delegated tasks. These leaders form part of the line management chain similar to that which you will be familiar with in the military.

Leadership can be demonstrated by anyone with responsibility within the workplace and it is this that separates it from management. Leaders can be relatively basic grade staff but who have a specific role to lead or co-ordinate or oversee a particular work practice. Leaders also come in all shapes and sizes and there are leaders you will be able to relate to and those you won't. In some workplaces you don't need to be able to demonstrate too much skill and knowledge to be given a leadership role; this might be quite different to what you are used to in the military. Some organisations provide internal leadership training programmes, whilst others offer external programmes, for example accredited with the CMI or ILM. But there are others for which leadership training is not a requirement to obtain a leadership role, and this again is something that might seem at odds with your previous experience. We are not advocating for one leadership and management method and structure over another, but we do feel that it's important that you are aware that you are likely to experience some significant differences in how civvy organisations differ and how they might be quite distinct from what you have experienced previously. This brings us on to a real-life comparison.

MILITARY AND CIVILIAN WORKPLACE COMPARISON

We've already suggested that you're likely to find some significant differences in the culture of any future workplace compared to that of the military. In the passage below, Richy offers a valuable account of his experiences of working both in the military and in a civilian role. This is a useful insight into two quite different work cultures. Bear in mind whilst reading this that there will be some civilian employers and organisations that do share some similarities to the military.

In some ways, the military has adapted and evolved much quicker and faster to political and policy changes than the civilian workplace. This might be due to the MoD being directly funded by the Government as opposed to other public services being funded (at least partly) by the local authorities. This close relationship to the Government may give the sense that working in the military is quite different to any civilian workplace. In the military there is a culture of being keen and prompt in seeking Government approval and closely following Government direction. The military operates a strong authoritarian work protocol, and this is played out by a strict hierarchy that demonstrated in the way one addresses colleagues (Sir, Ma'am etc) and in saluting when necessary. Officers enforce and 'order' their subordinates to comply with their commands and policies. There are no Trade Unions or statutory professional organisations that influence professional standards etc. in the military.

Speaking from the experience of 22 years in the British Army, the system of practice is a very authoritarian style of direction, leadership and 'guidance'. If you are told to be somewhere or on a particular course or duty . . . then you must be there, on time and willing to take direction. That's not to say this is not a fair system; care and consideration is exercised on scheduling duties, for example, you would not be placed on weekend Guard Duty continuously. However, about working shifts, military personnel frequently work shifts of over eight hours; these shifts are carried out according to the military's own guidelines that stipulate times within the shifts for rest and meal breaks. The training and learning environment in the military is similar to the work environment in that teaching is very direct and authoritarian. Some military training courses could be perceived as being quite blunt and harsh, and some programmes are physically and mentally extremely tough and demanding, for example, the Para and Royal Marine qualifications courses. The methods of teaching and delivery on these courses is very direct and blunt. You very rarely hear any "please" or "thank you" from the instructors, but as the military prides itself on camaraderie and loyalty, instructors are inclined to be 'fair but firm' and provide the highest quality of instruction and diligence . . . often taking the time and effort to repeat training scenarios or go over many of the often complex and demanding lessons and qualifications in their own time. It is no secret or surprise that the military can be blunt and sometimes brutal when it has to be, but I think most people in the military and Veterans will say that it works well and achieves its aim, that of 'keeping the troops happy.'

In comparison, then, to working and learning on Civvy Street, one of the first things I noticed was the lack of response to communication and requests for information. Having to work with civilian human resource departments has, in my experience, been frustrating and annoying in terms of the speed and content of reply to my request for basic information. Being able to have trade union and human resource representation and support in an occupation may be advantageous, but it can also be frustrating and challenging as these departments have their own ways of working and, seemingly, their own time schedules.

Another big difference I felt was the "9 to 5" culture of the civilian workplace. Of course, most military work procedures don't fall neatly into a "9 to 5" routine so this took some getting used to. I also felt, in some workplaces, that the way the employer supports, and trains new staff is nothing like the amount of support given to new people in the military. My experience was of a workplace that didn't promote a particularly supportive environment for new staff. The way the new staff were spoken to and treated was much different to the military; this may sound very odd to state but although the military are direct there is still a very humanitarian and compassionate side to commanders, who seemed to understand their subordinates and sympathise with them, for example in offering time away for a family problem.

So, as you can see, there are some significant differences between working in the military and working for a civilian employer, but there will also be some similarities. We reiterate what we have discussed previously and go on to discuss in the next chapter, that when you are applying for Civvy jobs or looking to work in a particular sector, do plenty of research on that organisation and find out as much as you can about it before you commit yourself. We discuss the three key work sectors in much more detail in the next chapter, but since the Covid pandemic, each of the work sectors are likely to be affected significantly in terms of how the working practices have had to change to meet the challenges that the restrictions have created.

POST-COVID WORKPLACES

Since the outbreak of the Covid pandemic in early 2020, workplaces, employers and employees have had to adapt rapidly to Government directives on how to continue to work safely and effectively. For many this has resulted in home working, which has provided some challenges, particularly for people and families having to home school children at the same time as working. The media has, at times, painted quite an "apocalyptic end of society" (O'Halloran 2020:10-11) in terms of how it has reported on the Pandemic; this has been largely driven by political forces. However, we suggest that where there are significant business and job losses, which is always unfortunate and, for some, life changing, there are also many opportunities and positive options. Working flexibly from home might well become more popular and some organisations have found that allowing staff this method of working has led to them being more productive. Using technology has also increased with virtual meetings, seminars, and even conferences becoming the working norm for some areas of industry. Depending which dimension you consider the implications that Covid has on organisations, will depend on whether you feel there are benefits or limitations. For example, the travel industry has struggled to maintain any momentum and has had to make redundancies as people are not permitted to travel. Similarly, universities have lost the income from international students and overseas research income, and so have been forced to restructure and, in some cases, merge faculties. On the other hand, there are areas that have benefited from the pandemic. Cyber has seen a significant increase in interest and job opportunities as we are using technology more which therefore creates the space for internet fraud. Similarly, logistics and courier services have witnessed an increase in service as people shop on-line much more. The question will be, whether these traits continue when the pandemic is controlled and to what degree. There may also be many more opportunities for franchises and self-employed business to develop as the reality of what will be required in the new word becomes evident. The Covid pandemic created a landscape of significant challenge as we've discussed, but prior to the outbreak of the pandemic, there were other challenges too.

WORKPLACE BARRIERS AND CHALLENGES

We've discussed many issues that you'll encounter in the civilian workplace and many benefits, and where we advocate that military veterans are an asset to the workforce and professional arena; we are also aware that some service leavers have reported various challenges when entering the civilian workplace. The veterans we spoke to whilst researching for this book enlightened us to the fact that there were occasions when they felt their journey to employment in Civvy Street wasn't as smooth as they had anticipated. These real-life stories correlate with a report in the Pathfinder Magazine (May 2020) that claims 30% of service leavers aged over 50 reported experiences of ageism and anti-military bias, or both, when job seeking in Civvy Street. However, the same report found that 40% of older service leavers reported that it was straightforward and relatively easy to secure employment in Civvy Street, and of these 85% found their new post interesting. In terms of ageism or age discrimination, it is important to add that treating someone unfairly because of their age is against the law in the UK – this is part of the Equality Act 2010. However, age discrimination is one of the most common forms of unfair treatment in the civilian workplace regardless of whether the employees are military veterans or not. The ACAS website is especially useful for information on age discrimination **www.acas.org.uk**

The issue of facing anti-military bias is complex and any such practice, if still evident, probably depends on the individual employer or organisation, or might even be the sole view of a particular manager within the organisation. The veterans' views that we sought when we were researching this book didn't identify any evidence of anti-military bias whatsoever; in fact two of the people we spoke to, one of whom became a police officer and the other a fire fighter, claim the fact they were military veterans was looked upon as a great advantage. Chris, the Police Officer, told us that he felt that the fact he had been in the military worked in his favour when he was recruited into the police force. It seems, then, that anti-military bias is not something that can be predicted nor confirmed. Matt, the firefighter, also felt that his military background was "a great asset" as he was able to embrace the hierarchy and team-work required by the fire service. Claire, an ex-Royal Navy nurse, spoke of her naval nursing experience being "both a benefit and a disadvantage" as she found it hard to adapt to nursing in the NHS. She spoke of a lack of discipline in the NHS that she found hard to comprehend. She did eventually find work in a private nursing home and felt "much happier with the way it was run and the degree of camaraderie between the staff".

SUMMARY

We have tried to offer an overview of the kinds of situations that you might experience in seeking for and working in organisations in Civvy Street. We have intentionally not gone into detail, although we are aware that there is much opportunity to do so. Look out for our book on *The Civvy Street work culture: Working in Civvy Street* where we do delve deeper into some of the issues you are likely to grapple with when considering a Civvy Job. The next chapter now looks at how you might prepare for and get a Civvy Street job.

REFERENCES

Argyle, M. (1989) *The Social Psychology of Work*. London. Penguin

Handy, C. (1991) *The Age of Unreason*. London. Century Business.

Handy, C. (1996) *Beyond Certainty*. London. Arrow

Mullins, L. (2002) *Management and Organisational Behaviour*. Essex. Prentice Hall.

O'Halloran, G. (2020) Post Covid19 – your Military operational skills could become essential to the business community. *Pathfinder*. May 2020

O'Shea, V. (2018) *Shaping your workplace culture: A practical guide*. Culture Shakers Publications.

Sturdy, J. (2020) Covid 19 – People are still recruiting and networking even in times of crisis. *Pathfinder*. April 2020. Pg. 14–15

CHAPTER 9

PREPARING FOR A NEW CIVILIAN CAREER

> "The outlook for service leavers moving into civilian employment is hugely positive. 81% of veterans find paid employment . . . more employers are becoming aware of the business benefits of investing in veteran recruitment"
>
> Lee Holloway (2018). Foreword to Veterans Work: Moving On. Downloaded from Veteranswork.org.uk

INTRODUCTION

In the previous chapter we looked at some key aspects of the civilian workplace and how changes to national policy and in society can influence the decisions employers make. Drawing on these previous discussions, we'll now look at how you can prepare yourself for a civilian occupation or prepare to set up your own business or franchise. Obviously, any detailed preparations will depend on the job you apply for, or business you are interested in developing, but there are some general principles that you can consider that will help you in your quest for a civilian career, and it is these that we focus on in this chapter. You may have made use of The Career Transition Partnership, in which case, you'll be familiar with the various career resettlement services in the military. However, we thought it might be useful to provide an overview here of the sort of things you should consider before applying for a job. Before you leave the military there are two things you can do that will significantly support any applications for employment in Civvy Street. Firstly, secure one or two opportunities for references from seniors within the military. Ask a few people if they are happy for you to contact them in the future for references for any job applications and get their contact details. Try to select people who know how you work and are likely to give you a good reference. The second thing you can do is to ensure you obtain your Certificate of Service that you should receive when you leave the service – make sure the military have the correct address to send this to once you leave. This certificate is the evidence that you have served and the length of time of your service; it also gives a profile of your competencies that could form an excellent basis for the skills section of your curriculum vitae that we explain later in this chapter.

We focus here on working in the UK, but we acknowledge that you may be considering working abroad. Several countries rate British military veterans very highly for certain trades and services. You will need to obtain specialist advice in terms of citizenship and visa considerations; you will also need to understand how your move may affect your pension. There are several sites that may be useful for information (**www.pathfinderinternational.co.uk www.armyandyou.co.uk www. citizensadvice.org.uk**), but we suggest that you start by understanding the latest UK Government advice on this (particularly since the COVID restrictions) on **www.gov.uk** (Ministry of Defence).

THE IMPACT OF COVID-19

The Covid pandemic led to the establishment of several Nightingale Hospitals across the UK. During the development of these hospitals, the media reported on the hugely significant role that the military played in ensuring these hospitals were up and running in a matter of weeks. This operation demonstrated to society and to civilian employers the skill sets that military personnel possess and threw a spotlight on how these could be beneficial in Civvy Street. For example, skills such as adaptability, team working, commitment and leadership were seen on the TV screens daily. This has enabled employers and managers responsible for recruiting and appointing staff to be more aware of the potential for employing ex-military personnel and where some companies and organisations have constricted and made redundancies, some going out of business completely, there are many more that are continuing to recruit. Some are even recruiting at a greater rate than before the pandemic. For example, it is well publicised that there is a national shortage of NHS healthcare workers and of prison custody staff. We believe that where the pandemic has sadly resulted in many job losses, it has created many opportunities for people with the skills that military leavers possess. The Pathfinder magazine (December 2019) suggested that the following job roles are likely to be in demand:

- **Care Worker** – In elderly care and in mental health and social care. There are also frequent job vacancies for support workers in the community. These roles are focused on supporting people to be able to live more independent lives.
- **Computer programming** – Software development and computer programming jobs are always advertised. Cloud storage and artificial intelligence vacancies are growing and similarly, business and gaming. It is difficult to imagine a time in the future when these roles will not be required in some significant number.
- **Data Analyst** – Engineering UK has estimated that 157,000 new jobs will be created across the UK in data analysis. Largely due to the increase in demand for the storage of such vast amounts of information about people and their preferences.
- **Construction workers** – The UK construction industry needs thousands of people every year to fill manual and non-manual roles. Carpenters, joiners, bricklayers, electricians and plumbers are always

sought after. This is likely to increase as during and immediately following the Covid-19 restrictions and because of BREXIT, foreign workers are not available in anything like the numbers that were seen prior to 2021.

- **Nurse –** A Health Foundation report published on 9th December 2020 found that there are significant shortfalls in the number of nurses. This coupled with the pandemic and the backlog of routine health care because of the Covid restrictions has led to the need to exceed the target for 50,000 new nurses by 2024.

- **Diagnostic Technician –** Vehicles are fitted with more and more electronics and gadgets. The diagnostic technician's job is to identify faults. With more electric vehicles coming onto the forecourt, it's probably safe to say that there will be more diagnostic technicians required in the future.

- **Cyber security –** This is a hugely growing sector. As cyber-based crime is on the increase, firms and businesses employ cyber specialists to support their IT and help prevent them from becoming victims of fraud.

- **Goods Vehicle drivers –** LGV and HGV drivers support the economy more than ever since Brexit and the Covid-19 pandemic. This sector has been understaffed for some time and there's no indication that this is improving. The logistics industry is always seeking new drivers.

- **Prison Officer –** The prison service is another sector that is always understaffed. If you were to search "vacant custody officer" and "prison officer" posts, there are not many prisons that would not feature in your search results as many prisons in the UK are understaffed.

- **Production Manager –** The manufacturing sector is always recruiting people with excellent leadership and management skills.

- **Fitness Instructor –** Search for personal trainer and fitness instructor vacancies and there will be numerous gyms and health suites that need posts filling.

- **Mechanical Engineer –** Good engineers are always in high demand. 200,000 people with engineering skills at level 3 and above will be needed every year in the UK through to 2024.

- **Teacher** – There is a national shortage of primary school teachers, particularly male teachers. The shortage subjects in secondary schools are: Science, maths, and modern foreign languages. Teaching is a degree profession, but there are a variety of routes in to teaching.

WORDS FROM THE HORSE'S MOUTH

Prior to writing this book and to enable us to provide you with real stories from veterans who have made the transition to working in Civvy Street, we interviewed several managers and people responsible for recruiting and appointing staff. Organisations represented in this sample were: NHS, Prison service, Private sector health and social care, Education and training, Retail and Agriculture, and farming. They all agreed that the pandemic has forced them to reconsider their recruitment strategy and their criteria for recruiting staff; most are focusing on appointing staff with quite different and diverse skills. They rated the following as "vital" skills for the future of the civilian workforce in the UK: *Adaptability and flexibility* were the main skills that were considered essential for new staff as working from home or across different locations was thought to be something that would be increasingly necessary. Two of the employers said that they would value adaptability and flexibility before anything else as they felt they promoted a resilience that was vital to future work ethic. *Strong communication and organisation skills* were also deemed essential as many organisations will restructure and many will be undergoing some sort of constant change. *Effective leadership and change management* were the other main attributes that employers will be seeking. We argue that these are all skills that military leavers possess in significant quantities. Later in the chapter we suggest how you might approach developing your CV. If these skills are thought to be vital by employers, then it might be worth reflecting on how you can demonstrate these.

WHERE ARE YOU GOING TO WORK?

We were struck by the conversations with some veterans regarding where they call "home". Paul, who served in the RAF spoke of being brought up in Dudley, but having lived "all over the world with the RAF" wouldn't consider Dudley his home, so when he retired, he wanted to live in the place that he felt held the happiest memories for him whilst in the RAF. So, he resettled to Oxford and that is where he lives and works today. Matt, a retired Navy warrant officer, was born and raised in Milton Keynes, and tells a similar story of retiring from the Navy in Portsmouth and "not giving a second thought to returning to Milton Keynes" despite his parents and family still living there. There is this issue, then, of where you will resettle to and the type of work available in that area.

If you're not sure of where you want to resettle and/or work, or the type of job you want to do, it might be worth starting with the list of all the organisations in that area that have signed the Armed Forces Covenant. You can get this list on **www.armedforcescovenant.gov.uk** By signing the covenant, these companies have signalled that they are supportive of the armed forces and have committed to treating military personnel and veterans fairly. However, you may know exactly the sort of job you want or the sector you want to work in and so will have a good idea of where to start. We talk later of employment and recruitment consultants, but these agencies also are good places to search for available jobs. There are several particularly good job search sites, for example:

- www.indeed.co.uk
- www.reed.co.uk
- www.totaljobs.com
- www.simplyhired.com

There will be others in your local area that focus on vacancies in that locality. Most of these sites provide a facility for you to upload your CV to the site and they match vacancies to your qualifications etc. We discuss the importance of the CV later in this chapter, but this is a good starting point to get yourself into the jobs market. LinkedIn is also another effective way of telling employers you are available for work and the type of work that you are looking for. You can set a jobs alert on LinkedIn that enables you to receive regular job vacancies that correspond to your search criteria. There are some job roles that are increasingly difficult to fill and so feature regularly on job sites. Since the Covid pandemic has resulted in several job losses in certain areas, it has created jobs in others. It is usually best to check out the website of the company you are interested in working for to identify if they have any vacancies.

Wherever you decide to search for work, your attitude to your prospective job and employer matters hugely. The Civilian workplace is quite different to anything you will have experienced in the military and if you approach it with an open mind and with a willingness to adapt you'll be more likely to be successful. We have already spent a large part of this book talking about your excellent skill set. We've also discussed how being confident about these skills and in recognising how they are transferable will be valuable to you in seeking a Civilian job. However, none of this will be of any use to you if you approach the job or employer with the wrong attitude.

ATTITUDES

Having served in the military, some of the skills and attributes you bring to any employment will be optimism, diligence, keenness, discipline, and excellent time keeping. You might be surprised, then, that civilian employees don't necessarily display these tendencies. It depends on the workplace, of course, and on the culture and management within that workplace. In some of the uniformed public services, there is a higher element of discipline and direction than in other occupations. The notion of attitude is a contested one that has led to psychological debate for some time. It is generally considered something to do with an evaluative behavioural response to someone, something, or an event. You will no doubt have come across many different types of attitudes within the military, both from your peers and from your managers, and so it is in Civvy Street. A common criterion on the person specification in job applications is about attitude to work and how you can demonstrate this. Similarly, one of the things a prospective employer might ask your referee (we discuss getting job references later) is about your attitude to work. So, this notion of attitude is quite relevant to working in Civvy Street.

Another distinct feature of the Military is the "dark" and "unique" sense of humour sometimes displayed by members of the forces. This is also sometimes prevalent in other uniformed civilian services and is thought to be used as a coping mechanism through challenging and difficult tasks. We are certainly not advocating that you should not see the humorous side of a situation, but in Civvy Street, any humour should be appropriate, measured and not offensive to anyone. The fact that you might find something inoffensive doesn't mean a colleague won't. You only need to read a newspaper to learn of sexism, bullying and abuse in the workplace. Many of these cases were taken to court as someone thought a conversation was a "bit of banter" when it was interpreted very differently by a colleague. Similarly, you may have shared "jokes" and humorous (to you) pictures and photos over social media and WhatsApp etc, but these might not be welcomed by some civilian colleagues. We would also suggest you exercise care when posting comments on social media (Facebook, Twitter etc) as some employers will watch their staff behaviour on social media in case they risk bringing the company into disrepute. Refrain from posting any comments and views on religion, politics, gender, or sex if possible, as these areas are very often contested and are a common reason for complaint.

Having been part of a disciplined and hierarchical service, you are familiar with taking orders and demonstrating respect. You will be no stranger to having to respond quickly and effectively to situations and directions. Don't be too surprised to find that some civilian employees might not demonstrate such keenness or appear quite so conscientious. In some companies, the employees may seem uninterested, unfocused, and even lazy and where this might be so, it's a matter of interpretation. The way you interpret these things is influenced by your experience; the way the civvy employee interprets things is influenced similarly by their own experiences, which will be quite different from yours. There are often heated debates in meetings, where employees might challenge managers; this is normal in some companies and is largely due to the way in which the companies are managed. Karen gives her view of a management culture she developed when she was the matron of a large nursing establishment:

I was the matron of a 67-bed nursing home that looked after young and elderly physically and mentally ill people. I was responsible and accountable for all the nursing care and for the management of 52 staff. It was, in my opinion, crucial that I established a leadership and management culture within the home. It was vital then that my management and leadership style supported and developed staff as well as ensured the best possible nursing care for all the clients. Nursing homes are regulated, and so regular inspections were carried out to ensure the quality of care. Having studied leadership and management, I was aware of different styles and methods of managing, but also, my own professionalism informed the type of manager I was. One of my biggest issues was and still is, the view that staff can tell you as a manager, what they think you want to hear – so, all the good stuff and how everything is fine and working well. Whether this was not to offend me or to try to keep me off their case, or something else, I don't really know; but for me, the first thing I wanted to know was when there was a problem, and the earliest I knew about it the better. So, I always encouraged my team to tell me as soon as possible when something had gone wrong, or whenever they made a mistake. This brings me on to something else: people make mistakes, and how you deal with that as a manager makes the difference between them being confident and effective team members, and being covert and devious, covering up errors. So, meetings I chaired were discussions and debates rather than me issuing directions and orders, and the staff were allowed to make mistakes. If we fast forward a few years, one of my recent managers (who held a very senior role) in a higher education establishment used to have a saying whenever he was met with some objection or challenge – "don't come to me with problems, come to me with solutions". I disagree wholeheartedly with this. My view is that it's his job as a manager to address and analyse the problems and to support the staff in finding solutions or to work on the solution himself. So, we were at odds for quite a bit of the time.

So, when you consider taking up a post in Civvy Street, or you consider working for yourself, the people you work for and with might have quite different views on how events and situations are managed. As we've said, you're coming at this from a certain perspective so might find others' responses difficult to understand.

The competitive nature of the military may still have an influence on you; after all, the motto of each of the services has a nod to the element of competition, but again, this might not be evident in the civilian organisation, and in some, might even be frowned upon. This is another reason to make sure you check out thoroughly the organisation or company to which you are considering applying. We will repeat this throughout this chapter as it is crucial to your success in finding an employer or organisation with whom or which you can effectively work. The civvy employment arena may appear to you to be much slower and less responsive than that which you are used to. There is certainly much more margin for error in certain occupations that you may have experienced in the past.

The rank you achieved in the military is not likely to have too much sway with the Civilian employer. It might be useful here to reflect on one of the interviews: Paul, the RAF Sergeant that we previously mentioned, told of a recent encounter. He recalled a conversation he had had with a Warrant Officer who was going through resettlement a couple of years after Paul and wanted to chat to Paul about his own experiences.

"This warrant officer thought that, because he'd held this rank in the RAF, he was guaranteed a senior manager's job when he left the service. Having been through the transition to Civvy Street myself and knowing many other people who have done the same, I was able to tell him that he's living in another world. I told him working in Civvy Street is a totally different kettle of fish and that he's not likely to be able to just walk into

such a senior job. The trouble is, they have this rank in the military, but they need to understand that they might not get a job with such a good status in Civvy Street."

It's a fine balance, then, isn't it? Your skills and experience will provide you with some good opportunities. You will be welcomed with open arms in some organisations and occupations. However, there may be others for which having Military experience is not so significant. How you present and project yourself makes a difference to how you will be accepted. This is the same for most other employees, too, regardless of whether they have been in the military or not. The balance here is drawing on your previous experiences and knowledge in a measured and balanced way and in a manner that is appropriate to the organisation and people within it. Be confident, you have earned it. But also, be careful in how you demonstrate this confidence. You may need to draw on self-confidence in different ways depending on what sort of civilian occupation you enter. For example, if you are working as part of the store team at B&Q, you might want to be a bit measured in terms of how you demonstrate your strengths; whereas, if you are starting your own business or setting up a franchise, you'll need to be strong in your self-belief. We'll discuss these different models of employment below.

WORKING FOR A CIVILIAN EMPLOYER – SOME INITIAL GENERAL OBSERVATIONS AND TIPS

In the months before leaving the military, you are provided with lots of information regarding resettlement from various sources. You need to try to understand all this as well as several forms that you need to complete and submit. You could be forgiven for feeling a bit overwhelmed by the amount of information and apparent advice that is on offer. However, it is important that you know there is a wealth of good information for you should or whenever you need it. It could be argued that after joining the military, leaving it is just as big a change for you to come to terms with. We signpost to many of the publications later in the book, but we thought it would be a good idea to emphasise some of the main considerations here.

When looking for work, some people find that sending their CV (Curriculum Vitae) to employment agencies or job consultants is a viable option. You might decide to try this method too. You'll need to make sure your CV is as good as it can be (we go into detail about this later in this chapter), and then send it to the job consultants that represent the sector you are interested in. So, for example, if you are considering working in the public sector, you might consider sending your CV to: **www.reed.co.uk www.hays.co.uk www.totaljobs.com www.indeed.co.uk** There will be other local recruitment agencies local to you that you should check out. Wherever you decide to work you'll need to present your P45 form and tell your new employer (or your accountant if working for yourself) about your tax contributions.

P45

One of the final things you'll need to sort out, towards the end of your resettlement period, is your P45. This will be generated by the pay department and sent to you following your final pay statement. It is important that you understand what is on your P45 and that you retain it securely as any future employer will need it before you commence work in a civilian role. The actual form contains details of your tax code, when you left the organisation, your total earnings up to that point, and how much tax you have paid. It contains personal information, too, like your name, date of birth and national insurance number. All employers are legally required to send you a P45, so if you don't receive it you should ask for it. There are four parts to the P45; you will receive three of these as part 1 will be sent from your previous employer to the tax office as official notification of you leaving the service. You need to retain part 1 of the form, as it'll be needed by your accountant or yourself, if you need to complete a self-assessment tax form (if you start up your own business or if you do self-employed work). When you take another employed job, then your new employer will need parts 2 and 3 of the P45. If you carry out any paid work and you've not been able to give your P45 to your new employer, you will be taxed on an emergency tax code until you can forward your P45 to them. If you don't immediately have a job to go to but you do intend to work, you might consider signing up at Job Centre Plus, in which case, you'll give them parts 2 and 3 of the P45. When you find a job, Job Centre Plus will bring your national insurance contribution record up to date prior to sending parts 2 and 3 to your new employer (Petley 2020). Never dispose of any parts of your P45 in the bin or in the recycled paper bin – it contains just the sort of information that fraudsters need. If you do need to get rid of it (and we can't think why this might be), burn it!

TAX

Working out how your tax affairs can be best managed once you leave the military can be complex. We advise that you get good financial advice so that you can understand these complexities and know exactly what your options are. Here, we discuss some of the basic tax issues that have been reported by Mary Petley (2020) of the Forces Pension Society.

Whatever you intend or decide to do in terms of working once you've left the military, you'll need to consider how your tax is managed. Any pensions and early departure payments count as "earned income" and are usually taxable, but you do not pay national insurance contributions in respect of them. The only exception to your pension not being subjected to tax is if you have been medically discharged with a condition that has been because of service and has given rise to compensation. It is worth checking the rate of tax as the Scottish rate is slightly different to the English rate of tax. As a guide, in 2020-2021 the English rates of tax are as follows:

- Up to £12,500 zero
- £12,501 – £50,000 20%
- £50,001 – £150,000 40%
- £150,001 45%

When you start working for a Civilian employer, you must tell the employer how much pension/early departure payment you receive in order that they can work out your tax liability. The same applies if you work for yourself – tell your accountant about your pensions.

The tax office dealing with your pension and early departure payments is:

Public Department 2, Ty-Glas, Llanishen, Cardiff, CF14 5QZ. Tel. **0300 200 3300**

SETTING UP YOUR OWN BUSINESS

If you are considering setting up your own business, it is worth considering the needs of your service or product in the geographical area in which you are thinking of establishing your business. The demand for certain services and products fluctuates depending on the area, so you'll need to research what your target area needs, now and in the future to ensure that your business is successful. Would you set up a business selling snow to Eskimos?

However, setting up your own business on leaving the military can be a real opportunity, particularly if you have a trade. The workplace has always been quite a changeable arena as different sectors have to adapt to respond to policy and legislative changes. But nothing prepared the world of work for the two biggest influences to manifest themselves concurrently in early 2020 – Brexit and the Covid-19 Pandemic. These two global events have hit some of industries hard, the Pathfinder magazine of September 2020 reports that the Construction industry suffered a significant decline in the spring and summer of 2020 but is expected to recover well. It is not yet fully realised how the sector's foreign workforce has been affected by Brexit and the pandemic, but opportunities for self-employed workers (architects, plumbers, electricians, joiners etc) could well increase significantly as building eventually returns to levels like that prior to the pandemic.

We would suggest that, if you are considering a self-employed business you need to start any business planning with energy and enthusiasm despite the Covid restrictions. But since Covid and Brexit, where there have been losses and declines in self-employed companies, there are also gains and opportunities, it could well be the smaller, self-employed freelance worker and the small enterprises that get the country back on its feet. So, if nothing you have read so far has put you off, the next part of this chapter aims to support you in some practical suggestions and in developing your thoughts further in terms of securing work in Civvy Street.

The following "Have you got what it takes" checklist has been adapted from Mike Johnson's book (2009) on starting up your own business. It's worth having a go at it as it gives you some idea of the skills you'll need to draw on if you're thinking of starting up on your own. Be very honest about yourself when you're completing these questions:

Have you got what it takes to start your own business?

Temperament	Score yourself 1 – 10 1 = low and 10 = high
I am self-motivated and able to multi-task	
I am willing to study and learn – attend college/ university if necessary	
I have strong perseverance skills	
I am able to tolerate uncertainty and risk	
I have, or will develop, good business and development networks	
I am able to draw on reliable people and have a supportive family/friends network	
I have strong physical and mental energy	
I have enough money in the bank to survive for at least six months	
I have excellent communication skills	
I have excellent time management skills	
I can transfer professional and knowledge skills	
My skills are not going to be obsolete in a couple of years	

On the basis of your score – this is what action is suggested you take now:

Under 60 – Don't try to work for yourself just yet. Find a job and/or take up a training course. But don't lose the idea. Use a year or so in another job to develop your idea of setting up yourself.

60 – 90 – Give this some serious thought. Develop the skill set you will need and start to work on each of the areas that you have a low score.

90 or over – Do it now!

This is just a quick guide, there are many more considerations and things you'll need to weigh up, but it's a decent starting point to get you thinking. Starting your own business is not easy – if it were everyone would be doing it – but you are starting from a really sound and strong foundation engineered in your years spent in the military. There's never enough time when you first start up. Those afternoons on the golf course or weekends away might have to be sacrificed for the first few months (or even years). Don't expect to be a success right away, all businesses take time to get established and to secure a position in whichever market-place they occupy. We advise you to seek out your local Chamber of Commerce. The Chambers are focused entirely on supporting local businesses, and where they differ in terms of how they carry out their responsibilities, it would be useful for you to identify if your local Chamber is able to support you. They charge a yearly fee for membership of the Chamber, for which you get access to rooms and meetings etc, and often, particularly good networking events. There may be other local business support groups that would be useful to you, so check these out. Your local authority would be a good place to start for this.

INITIAL THOUGHT ABOUT YOUR BUSINESS

So, you're seriously considering setting up your own business? Why? What is it that is driving you to want to work for yourself? Give this a lot of thought as you will need to be absolutely committed to the idea if you are to have any chance at succeeding. We might as well be very blunt at this stage: according to the Office for National Statistics (2019) roughly 80% of companies fail within their first year. This isn't meant to deter you, just to alert you to the statistics. These were reported prior to Brexit and the Covid pandemic; it will be interesting to see how these events have impacted on the rise and fall of businesses in the coming years. There are many reasons for people succeeding in starting a business against the odds: Passion in the idea or product, sheer hard work and resilient tenacity, not wanting to work for some soulless corporation etc. and you'll have your own similar ideas; don't lose sight of these as it is this that is likely to keep you going when the going gets tough.

One you've analysed your business idea and discussed it with people you trust and whose opinion you value, and you've thought of all the pros and cons, you'll need to start to develop your business plan. If you are needing to get a business loan from the bank, you'll probably need to present a business plan to the bank. Your bank will be able to provide you with a template for your plan, but you can also get templates from your Chamber of Commerce or download a copy. We have downloaded an example of a simple business plan below.

This is a simple document, and your business plan might look much more detailed, but this gives you an idea of what you need to be thinking about when planning your business. If you are going to need a business loan from your bank, they will need more information.

It is always good to have a mission for your business. So, for example, you might be starting up as a delivery driver. The service you provide will be a door-to-door delivery/courier service, but your mission might include an environmental impact, so you'll want to be clear that you are considering emissions etc. Knowing your competitors and how successful their businesses are is important. In order that you have a USP (unique selling point) you'll need to know how you can be unique, so knowing the opposition is key to your understanding of this. The other method of business or project planning is by using a Gantt chart. This is a tool for project management but can be usefully adapted for use as a business plan. There are various Gantt chart outlines available free on-line.

Business plan example: downloaded from: **www.smartsheet.com**

ONE PAGE BUSINESS PLAN FOR A SERVICE BUSINESS TEMPLATE

BUSINESS OVERVIEW	
OUR VISION	
OUR MISSION	
THE SERVICE WE PROVIDE	

MARKET ANALYSIS	
WHO WE ARE TARGETING	
THE PROBLEM WE ARE SOLVING	
OUR COMPETITORS	
OUR COMPETITIVE ADVANTAGE	

MARKETING AND SALES PLAN	
MARKETING CHANNELS	
MARKETING MATERIALS	
CUSTOMER INCENTIVES (REFERRALS, DISCOUNTS, ETC.)	
STAFF REQUIREMENTS/ TRAINING	

KEY OBJECTIVES AND SUCCESS METRICS	
OBJECTIVES WE PLAN TO ACHIEVE IN A GIVEN TIMEFRAME AND HOW THEY'LL BE MEASURED	
1	
2	
3	

Timeline of Milestones

Start 2/08	Milestone 2 02/16	Milestone 4 02/23	Milestone 6 03/03
Milestone 1 02/11	Milestone 3 02/20	Milestone 5 03/01	

When you've completed your business plan, and engaged with the bank if that is what you need to do, you'll need to consider cash flow.

CASH FLOW

The Pathfinder magazine of December 2019 suggested that, if you are considering setting up a business on leaving the armed forces, you need to consider cash flow. This is a real or virtual movement of money within your business. In the simplest sense, a cash flow can be the payment from one bank account to another. However, in business, the term "cash flow" usually describes the payments that are expected in the future. These are, of course, uncertain, so you need to forecast what these are likely to be – this is your cash flow. Your bank or accountant will help you to perform cash flow analyses if these are required. The Pathfinder report (2019) suggested various tips on improving your cash flow; these include:

Lease, don't buy	Leasing can have many benefits over buying. Check out the full range of these for specific items and services online.
Offer discounts on loans	Offer clients discounts for paying early or on time, this always helps with cash flow.
Conduct customer credit checks	Do your homework on clients (particularly if they are buying significant products or services from you) BEFORE doing business with them. A company with poor credit can have a detrimental effect on your cash flow.
Improve your inventory	Goods, products, and services that don't sell tie up money. Be ruthless here, sell for a discount rather than keep stock that does not sell and be prepared to change your service focus if necessary.
Send invoices out immediately	Do not wait to send invoices out. This creates slow payments, which again negatively impacts on cash flow.
Use electronic payments	Using electronic payments can save valuable time. They can also be more secure than paper-based records and invoices.
Pay suppliers less	This is a reverse of point 2. So, pay your suppliers early and on time and push for some discount for doing so. You won't be the only one doing this, but they won't tell you!

Use high interest savings accounts	This may sound obvious, but in the long term, this will help with liquidity (the conversion of assets into cash).
Increase pricing	Do not be afraid to raise your prices. Your business plan may have incorporated a yearly price review (if not, maybe it's an idea) so that your clients are aware of the potential for increases to costs.

This is really a considerably basic introduction to cash flow and the business planning. There are plenty of business start-up support groups that you can tap into. Don't be afraid of contacting them to introduce yourself and asking for help – that's what they are there for.

FRANCHISING

Similar in a way to starting up your own business, is taking on a franchise. Reed.co.uk offer the following information on franchising. Franchising is when an established business allows a third party the right to operate using their trade name. This is usually in return for a one-off franchise fee and a percentage of sales revenue. There are three types of franchise: Business format franchise, where a business (franchisor) licenses another business (franchisee) to trade using its business model and branding etc. The Franchisor may also offer other support products and training etc. This is the most common form of franchise in the UK. Secondly, there is a Product distribution franchise; this is where the franchisor allows the franchisee to sell its products. The franchisor will not provide any on-going support. An example of this is branded petrol stations. Thirdly, a manufacturing franchise is licensed to produce goods and services using the franchisor's brand name. For example, food and beverage companies – selling syrup concentrate to a bottling company which then sells it on after mixing (**www.reed.co.uk**).

WHY START A FRANCHISE?

This offers the opportunity to trade under a well-established name, which gives you a good start for your business and the contacts and networks (and clients) are already established. You also benefit from all the advertising and marketing that the franchisor carries out. Other benefits include dedicated and proven business model, focused support, on-going advice and guidance, and continual training. You may also be able to negotiate reduced buying costs and increased funding options due to the power and marketability of the brand. Successful franchises can be very lucrative.

LIMITATIONS AND RISKS OF A FRANCHISE

There are several things to consider before taking on a franchise. The first thing to give a lot of thought to is the financial commitment. You will need to "buy in" to the franchise. This is usually an initial payment. There may be payments required from you for other products from the franchisor, so you'll need to make sure that you are aware of this before you sign any agreement or contract. Then the franchisor will want a percentage of your profit – this again will need to be agreed. You may have to work long hours, at least initially, but probably for a considerable time, to get your franchise established. You need to make sure that being a franchisee is the right thing for you and your family, and that it fits with your career aspirations and motivations. There might not be room for you to be too creative in terms of making changes as you'll have to fit in with the franchisor's ethos and business objective.

Franchising can be a really good way to start your own business without having the stress and risk of going it totally alone. There are a variety of franchises available and some very much suited to service leavers and veterans. To find out more about franchise opportunities, check out **www.franchisedirect.co.uk**

WORKING IN THE PUBLIC SECTOR

We have discussed some of the features of the public sector in the previous chapter, but here we focus on what working in the public sector is like. The public sector is made up of organisations owned by the Government and generally provides a service for all citizens. Organisations in the public sector do not normally seek to generate profit. The office for National Statistics has reported that there are over 300 different occupations within the public sector and around 5.4 million people working across the sector (ONS 2019). They are working in jobs such as: teaching, nursing, paramedics, librarians, and armed forces personnel (as you well know). The public sector has a much higher percentage of high skilled jobs that that of the private sector. This is probably due to a large proportion of jobs requiring a degree. The Office for National Statistics is a useful resource to learn more of the public sector should you want to. Many of the organisations within the sector have had to respond quickly to the Covid pandemic. For example, NHS, schools and colleges, universities and local authorities, these organisations have had to adapt rapidly to unimaginable change. The media attention has shone a light onto the staff shortages in many of the public sector organisations. Buswell (2020) argues that service leavers could be the answer to the NHS staff shortage. He reports that the NHS is around 43,000 nurses short and 10,000 medically qualified staff. Nine out of ten hospital executives in England have reported that staffing shortages will pose risks to patient health. Since the Covid pandemic, these figures, sadly, are not likely to improve. In the past the NHS has recruited from abroad, but since BREXIT, this is not a viable proposition. For service leavers interested in a career in the NHS, a programme exists that is tailored specifically. The Military Step into Health programme is aimed at supporting service leavers into NHS occupations; it's worth checking out if you might be interested in a career in health. **www.militarystepintohealth.nhs.uk**

Similarly, the teaching shortage was the driver behind the Troops to Teachers programme which was a similar Government incentive to attract service leavers and veterans into teaching. This programme has now been discontinued. However, there are new incentives that are designed to attract service leavers into teaching; check these out on **www.getintoteaching. education.gov.uk**

Working in some public sector organisations may provide some similarities to the military in terms of having a structured hierarchy and being part of a uniformed service etc. But as we've said before and will continue to do so, do your homework on any prospective employer before you waste time filling in application forms etc.

WORKING IN THE PRIVATE SECTOR

As we mentioned in the previous chapter, the private sector organisations are made up of companies and businesses that are privately owned, either by individuals or by partnerships etc. The private sector is made up of all sorts of organisations of all shapes, sizes, and cultures and, as with the public sector, if you are considering working in the private sector, you should check out the company as thoroughly as possible before you spend time applying for any posts. In the third quarter of 2020 there were approximately 26.96 million people working in the private sector in the UK (Clark 2021). There are some significant differences to working in the public sector. The private sector is a very different culture, demonstrating quite distinct values, objectives, and attitudes. Organisations in the private sector interact with clients, staff, and customers quite differently too; this is largely due to the focus being on making a profit and less on delivering a service. Working in this sector can be very satisfying and exhilarating, depending on what you want from a job. There are no shortages of challenges and of reward in this sector, and private employers have great flexibility around how they pay and reward good staff. Some workers in the private sector speak of finding it more "personal" than the public sector and less hierarchical. If you live in a remote or rural area, there is probably more likelihood of there being more private employers near to you than public employers, so if location is an issue, you might find working in the private sector more practical.

WORKING IN THE THIRD SECTOR

The Third Sector is an umbrella term used to describe a range of organisations that cannot be categorised as either public sector or private sector. It includes employment areas such as: Housing associations, charities, social enterprises, and private research institutes. This sector is sometimes referred to as "not for profit" or "the voluntary sector". It is an employment area that allows you to work for a cause that is close to your heart or to work towards a change that you feel strongly about. It can be very motivating and satisfying working in this sector. In June 2018, 865,916 people worked in the third sector (NCVO 2018) which is 3% of the total UK workforce. The sector has grown more than 11% in the last eight years and considering the likely impact of the pandemic onto charities, we would argue that there is a considerable likelihood that this sector will grow in the future. Furthermore, the skills that service leavers have are tailormade for this sector and if we draw on the conversations in the earlier chapter regarding transferable skills, it seems sensible to suggest that your skill set would be an advantage should you consider applying, for example for a post with an international charity. But as with the other sectors, we cannot stress highly enough that you should do considerable research prior to committing to working in this sector.

NETWORKING

Once you leave the military it is understandable that you will feel a sense of loss. We speak much more about this in the next chapter, but you're bound to experience a shock to your senses. A particularly good way of counteracting any sense of isolation or vulnerability is to join or form a network of like-minded individuals. You may have links with other service leavers and veterans that you can draw on, maybe regiment associations etc. As this chapter is focused on civilian employment, we're concerned with networking for future career opportunities. "Networking is still, by far the best way to find a new role. You must continue leveraging your contacts, working LinkedIn and looking for employers who have signed the armed forces covenant" (Sturdy 2020: 14-15). You can't really network too much. It's very tempting, though, to focus your networking efforts on sticking to people you know from the Military or who are veterans, but like the saying goes: If you always do what you've always done, you'll always get what you've always got. So, in other words, nothing will change much. There are civilian individuals and organisations that will "get" your plight and will help you and support you. Don't dismiss these as they could be your gateway to a successful transition and career on Civvy Street. They're likely to already have networks in the Civilian sectors that you need introductions to. Nurture any Civvy contacts you have; they might be able to make a real difference to your transition and resettlement.

THE PRACTICAL BIT OF APPLYING FOR A JOB ON CIVVY STREET

Having discussed some of the key considerations you'll be addressing when applying for a civilian job, we now want to talk you through some of the practicalities of applying for a role as an employee. There are some variations to this, but largely the main issues are remarkably similar, and we set these out here.

ANSWERING THE JOB ADVERT

It is likely that the first thing you will know about the vacant job is either an email from a recruitment consultant (that you have previously sent your CV to) or a job advert on LinkedIn or on the company's website (if you are interested in a particular job type, then keep your eye on the companies' websites in that area). Read the job advert carefully and make sure, at this point, that you want to continue as this can now become a time-consuming exercise. But let's assume that you read the job advert on the organisation's website and you want to go for it. Somewhere on the advert it will ask you to either contact a person for an informal discussion and/or apply on-line. If you get the opportunity to contact a named person, **DO IT!** This is your opportunity to find out about the culture of the organisation and to give you an early indication if you could be a good fit. This is also your opportunity to get on the company's radar as being someone who is really interested in the company and keen to work with them etc. Prepare your questions prior to the discussion and listen to the answers carefully. This is not an interview – you do not need to tell them how good you are, neither should you start a discussion about your limitations. This is an opportunity for you to find out if it is the company for you and to give them a positive first impression of you. Once you've had this discussion you'll have a fairly good idea if you want to continue with the application, of which there are normally four parts.

Having worked in management roles where she has recruited staff to all grades both in the public and private sector, Karen now sets out the key considerations for a good application form, CV, covering letter and Interview – the four main stages of a job application.

Application form

The application form is your first opportunity to convince the employer that they need to interview you for the job. Application forms normally ask you to provide your personal details, education history, qualifications, memberships of professional bodies, professional history and then some specific details of skills that are required for the specific job. You will also need to supply the details of at least two people whom the employer will contact for a reference. Choose these people carefully and, if you can, have people with some credibility; the form will stipulate whether one of these needs to be your previous employer. On your application form pay particular attention to the way you report on skills specific to the job. Reflect on those skills that you have built up whilst in the Military and that are transferable and say this on the form. Firstly, read, and read again the job description. This is what you will be doing when you get the job, and the employer wants to know if you are able to do it. So, for example, the application form

*might ask for "excellent communication and interaction skills and abilities".
Reflecting on the first part of this – excellent communication skills – you will
need to explain what communication skills you are able to demonstrate,
why these are excellent and prove this by discussing a situation when you
have used them. Always justify what you say by giving an example. Anyone
can say that they are brilliant at conversation etc. But to give an example
puts this into context for the employer so that they can see how you have
been able to demonstrate it in a practical situation. Then the next part of
the question is about interaction skills. This gives you the opportunity to say
how you interact – so, writing, negotiating, persuading etc. If you struggle
to unpick the questions, go back to what the job description says and think
what interactions you will be likely to need to demonstrate. Don't rush this
part of the application, it's very often this section that makes the difference
between you getting shortlisted for the interview and being disregarded.
Don't leave the application form until the day before the deadline, give
yourself a chance to go over it a couple of times for spelling errors and other
corrections. You might have a friend you can ask to go over it for you. Once
you've completed the application form, you will need to complete a covering
letter to accompany the application form and a curriculum vitae (CV).*

Covering Letter

*Most job applications ask for a covering letter, but some hint that it is an
option. **THIS IS NOT AN OPTION**! If you want to be considered for the job,
make sure you complete a covering letter to accompany the application form
and your CV. Very often you are asked to write your cover letter on a blank
piece of paper/word document and this is where some people go wrong. Do
not be tempted to write a story of how good you will be for the company, or
how much you want the job. Use the **person specification** that will be part
of the application form/information together with the job description to
structure your cover letter. The person specification will identify exactly what
skills, knowledge and understanding you need to do the job. Some person
specification forms identify how these skills will be assessed at recruitment –
so for example they might say: A = application form and I = interview. Where*

this is the case, you'll have an idea what to expect at your interview. Using the criteria on the person specification form, then, you can begin to structure your covering letter. I would go so far as to suggest you use the exact wording on the person specification for your cover letter, so if one of the criteria was: "demonstrate advanced leadership skills in challenging situations", I would copy and paste this onto your cover letter and then go on to demonstrate how you have done this in a given situation. Then repeat this method for each of the criteria on the person specification. Once you've done this you will have an extraordinarily strong commentary of how you meet all the criteria needed for the job. At the end of the cover letter, I would also suggest you include a couple of sentences on how the skills you've built up in the Military are transferable to this post. Don't let anyone try to convince you that you don't need a cover letter.

Curriculum Vitae

Your Curriculum Vitae or CV is your shop window. It is a document that allows you to showcase your skills in a concise and clear manner so that employers can see briefly what your fundamental skills and professional experiences are. Your CV should be no longer that two sides of A4. It should be written in a clear and plain font and be easy to read. There are some good examples of CV templates on-line and by searching for "professional cv template" you have access to lots of good examples. There are a couple of tips for completing your CV:

- *Clearly identify your qualifications and work experience (but not in too much detail and start from the most recent at the top)*
- *Identify your key skills. (Make sure these are brief and that they are real skills, so: leadership, team building, driving etc. Don't leave the employer to assume anything – for example, "Afghanistan" is a country not a key skill, so you'll put the skills you demonstrated in Afghanistan rather than assuming the employer will know this.)*
- *You don't really need to include too much personal stuff; the employers aren't too bothered about hobbies and pastimes.*

To summarise, then, the CV and cover letter are vital documents to support your application. Take time over completing them. Don't let your CV gather dust, so every time you take a training programme then make sure you include it on your CV.

Preparing for the interview

You've completed your application form and cover letter and submitted them along with your CV by the deadline for the job applications. Now you just wait for your shortlisting notification. If you hear nothing, you have not been shortlisted. Do not be disheartened, you may be up against strong opposition that includes internal candidates. Don't let this prevent you from continuing to apply for other jobs, use it as experience. If you do get shortlisted, give yourself credit for a significant achievement.

The notification of interview should tell you when and where the interview will be and what the panel (you might be told who is on the panel) wants you to do. If you are informed who is on the panel, check them out on LinkedIn or find out who they are in the business and try to find out a bit about them. Then prepare for the interview. Depending what the job role is, determines what you will be asked to do at the interview – you might be asked to present on a subject. If so, you'll probably be given a length of time for the presentation; make sure you stick to this time, so prepare your presentation and test it out plenty of times prior to the actual interview. It might be that the panel will ask you a series of questions. One of the best things you can do to prepare for this type of interview is to get your head around the organisation's strategic objectives, values, mission statements etc, as there is normally a question or two to test if you know anything about the company. Some popular interview questions are:

- *Why do you want this job?*
- *What do you bring to this job/company?*
- *Tell me of a time when you have had to manage a difficult situation involving . . .*
- *Tell me of a time when you have had to negotiate within a conflict.*

- *What are your strengths?*
- *What are your limitations?*
- *What is your view of our company's values?*

Remember, that the employer needs to know whether you are the right person for the job. However, you also want to find out if they are the right employer for you, so when they ask if you have any questions, always have a couple of questions ready. These could be:

- *When are you likely to be able to confirm who has the job?*
- *What training opportunities are there?*
- *Is the starting salary negotiable?*

Since the Covid restrictions, employers have had to interview for staff via virtual meetings. These can offer some advantages over face-to-face, but also some disadvantages.

Try to get your head round using Zoom and TEAMS and other interview and presentation software. Try it out several times with a mate before the actual interview so that you can be as confident as possible with the technology. When you take part in the interview, look directly into the camera, not on the faces of the panel on your screen, that way, you're looking them in the eye. If you have made some notes as prompts, stick them on the edge of your monitor, don't let the panel see them.

When face-to-face interviews resume, enter the interview room, make eye contact with each of the panel and make a mental note of their names when introduced. Let the chair of the panel lead, they'll tell you how the interview will be carried out and let you know when you speak. Don't be tempted to interview the panel or command the interview.

COPING WITH THE INTERVIEW OUTCOME

Once you've taken part in the interview, you've done all you can to land the job. Now it's just a matter of waiting for someone to contact you to tell you whether you've got the job. If you've been successful, you'll be told what your next steps are and will be directed by the employer to what you need to do from this point on. If you are not successful, don't be too disappointed. Coping with rejection from employers is routine to a lot of people in Civvy Street, but it's probably not something you've had to manage. Don't take an unsuccessful interview to heart; it's not been a decision taken against you personally, it's just that you were not, apparently, the right person for the job on the day. But employers do get it wrong from time to time, so you may be contacted later asking if you were still interested in the job.

SUMMARY

This chapter has offered some signposts and suggestions for you to consider regarding a civilian career and resettling to work on Civvy Street. It is by no means the complete guide to this area but has provided some points for you to investigate further if you should need to. Civilian organisations differ enormously, even companies delivering similar services can have quite different cultures. Research the area you are interested in and particularly the specific company you are thinking of joining. Use social media to check up on the managers at the company and get a feel for the sorts of people they are. The time you spend in doing this research will be invaluable. Try not to be tempted to work in a particular place just because your mate works there – it might seem like a good idea (and for some of you it may well work) but working at a particular place for that reason is rarely successful in the long term.

REFERENCES

Buswell, G. (2020) Can Service leavers resuscitate the NHS? *Pathfinder* February 2020

Clark, D. (2021) Working in the Private sector. Statitsa. www.statista.com

Johnson, M. (2009) *Starting up on your own*. London. Prentice Hall

Ministry of Defence (2020) *Service Leavers' Guide.* www.gov.uk

Ministry of Defence (2015) *Information for Service Leavers.* www.gov.uk

National Council Voluntary Organisation [NCVO] (2018)

Office for National Statistics (2018) www.ons.org

Petley, M. (2020) Let's talk about Tax. *Pathfinder* magazine. P8 – 9

Petley, M. (2020) What is a P45 and what do I do with it? *Pathfinder* July 2020

Sturdy, J. (2020) Covid 19 – People are still recruiting and networking even in times of crisis. *Pathfinder.* April 2020

Weiss, A. (2016) *Million Dollar consulting.* New York. McGraw Hill.

CHAPTER 10

SUMMARY AND EPILOGUE

We hope that this book has provided some useful information for you, or for you to pass on to other service leavers or veterans and their families. There are changes happening to policy that impacts on service leavers regularly, so we reiterate our suggestion that you maintain regular access to the Government website and MOD communications for veterans for the most up to date information.

We have touched on some of the main areas that veterans and service leavers told us were important to them, and we have tried to explore some of the support opportunities around these areas. But there are some common threads running through conversations and discussions we've had and that we've tried to analyse. Firstly, we've discussed living in Civvy Street and some of the main issues and events that are likely to impact on you in terms of housing and health. Secondly, we looked at training in Civvy Street and how your military past can be beneficial in terms of picking up a college or university course; and thirdly, we have picked up on some of the key considerations for working on Civvy Street, where we've delved a bit into the culture of the civilian workplace. We have heard first-hand from some service leavers how their resettlement influenced and impacted on them and used their anecdotes to inform much of the discussions in the book. We encourage you to explore civilian networks and organisations that may support your resettlement and transition to Civilian life.

MISSING IT ALREADY?

This book is obviously focused on integrating back into Civvy Street, but for some of you this integration might be supported by maintaining some links with the military. If you still want to "keep your hand in" there are several ways in which you can maintain links with the military. The MOD introduced the service for experienced, re-joiner and volunteer engagement (SERVE) to enable you to discover wider opportunities within the military and stay connected.

If you are leaving the Army there are two main types of commitment: **Full commitment** – these fill regular army jobs that cannot be filled using regular personnel. The pay and conditions are like that of the regulars. The length of service will vary but should be clearly identified in the job advert. **Home Commitment** – these are established FTRS posts. These are initially for a maximum of three years and the pay and conditions vary from the full commitment posts. If you are interested in either of these, the details are on the Army Reserve page as **www.army.mod.uk**. Entry to any reserve service depends on your military service and the nature of discharge, so it's worth finding out if you can engage in any reserve service if that is an option that you are interested in.

If you are leaving the RAF but considering re-joining, maybe to put the skills you have already learnt, back to use or even to take up a completely different role, there are often positions open to you. Each application to re-join is looked at individually and considered on its own merits. You apply through the Defence Recruiting System (DRS). You can get advice on re-joining the RAF on tel: **0345 605 5555** or at **www.raf.mod.uk** on the re-joiners and inter-service transfer page.

If you are leaving the Navy and considering re-joining, you will need to be under the age of 37 to re-join the Royal Marines and under 50 to re-join the Royal Navy. There are high priority roles for which re-joiners may be considered. Each application is considered on its own merit and application forms and details of priority roles can be found at: **www. royalnavy.mod.uk** on the page "Served once, serve again".

The SERVE jobs list can be found on: **www.findforcesjobs.mod.gov.uk**

It's also worth remembering that on leaving full-time service, personnel are transferred into the reserves. This period of reserved service (albeit non participatory) usually lasts for a determined length of time and it's worth checking to see how long you will remain on the reserve list. Each of the three forces may call up reserves for long periods during emergencies, or when there is a "national need" as judged by the Defence Secretary (forces watch briefing **www.parliament.uk** "Terms of service in the UK Armed Forces"). There is useful and detailed information on **www.gov.uk** "Rights and Responsibilities for reservists and employers" regarding reservist call up and financial support for the employer that is worth reading.

There are also roles within the cadet force. These are usually (paid) instructor roles and the details can be found on:

https://armycadets.com/
https://www.raf.mod.uk/aircadets
https://www.royalnavy.mod.uk/our-organisations/cadets-and-youth

Before we sign off, we would like to thank you for taking the time to read this book, either in its entirety or in part, and hope that the information has gone some way to support your resettlement or to assist any queries you have about living, training, or working on Civvy Street.

EPILOGUE

As we mentioned at the start of the book, and throughout, the real-life stories from service leavers and veterans have been fundamental to increasing our understanding of the real and practical resettlement issues faced by military personnel and some of the challenges faced by veterans. We want to pay special tribute to one of these veterans. Chris served in the Parachute Regiment before joining the Police force. He knew what we were aiming to do in this book and he wholeheartedly supported our aims. He wanted his story to be heard as he felt that it may help other military service leavers and veterans. We have therefore drawn on Chris's anecdotes throughout the book. So, it is with a very heavy heart and great sadness that we learned during the writing of the book of Chris's passing. We dedicate this Epilogue to Chris.

Stricta Miles Somnum.

FURTHER BOOKS IN THE CIVVY STREET SERIES:

There are three more books in the Civvy Street series; these are:

- Living and working on Civvy Street.
- Training and studying on Civvy Street.
- Recruiting in Civvy Street: An employer's guide to taking on military veterans.

In subsequent books we explore in much more detail the aspects of each of these resettlement opportunities. We draw on research and theory to support some of the key arguments surrounding these themes and look much more critically at some of the experiences of veterans and people going through resettlement.